# COMMUNITY IN TRANSITION

**Recent Titles in**
**Contributions in Sociology**

Promises in the Promised Land: Mobility and Inequality in Israel
*Vered Kraus and Robert W. Hodge*

Switzerland in Perspective
*Janet Eve Hilowitz, editor*

Rethinking Today's Minorities
*Vincent N. Parrillo, editor*

Beyond Ethnocentrism: A Reconstruction of Marx's Concept of Science
*Charles McKelvey*

The Community in Rural America
*Kenneth P. Wilkinson*

The Next Three Futures: Paradigms of Things to Come
*W. Warren Wagar*

Changing Jewish Life: Service Delivery and Planning in the 1990s
*Lawrence I. Sternberg, Gary A. Tobin, and Sylvia Barack Fishman, editors*

Alienation, Community, and Work
*Andrew Oldenquist and Menachem Rosner, editors*

High Risk and High Stakes: Health Professionals, Politics, and Policy
*Earl Wysong*

Immigration and Ethnicity: American Society—"Melting Pot" or "Salad Bowl"?
*Michael D'Innocenzo and Josef P. Sirefman, editors*

The Poverty Debate: Politics and the Poor in America
*C. Emory Burton*

Diffusion Research in Rural Sociology: The Record and Prospects for the Future
*Frederick C. Fliegel*

Consciousness and Culture: An Introduction to the Thought of Jean Gebser
*Eric Mark Kramer, editor*

# COMMUNITY IN TRANSITION

## Mobility, Integration, and Conflict

Hanna Ayalon, Eliezer Ben-Rafael,
and Abraham Yogev



Contributions in Sociology, Number 104

GREENWOOD PRESS
Westport, Connecticut • London

**Library of Congress Cataloging-in-Publication Data**

Ayalon, Hanna.
Community in transition : mobility, integration, and conflict / Hanna Ayalon, Eliezer Ben-Rafael, and Abraham Yogev.
p. cm.—(Contributions in sociology, ISSN 0084-9278 ; no. 104)
Includes bibliographical references and index.
ISBN 0-313-28699-X (alk. paper)
1. New towns—Israel—Case studies. 2. Social planning—Israel—Case studies. 3. City planning—Israel—Case studies. 4. Social integration—Israel—Case studies. I. Ben Rafael, Eliezer. II. Yogev, Abraham. III. Title. IV. Series.
HT169.57.I75A93 1993
307.1'68'095694—dc20 92-20063

British Library Cataloguing in Publication Data is available.



Library of Congress Catalog Card Number: 92-20063
ISBN: 0-313-28699-X
ISSN: 0084-9278

First published in 1993

Greenwood Press, 88 Post Road West, Westport, CT 06881
An imprint of Greenwood Publishing Group, Inc.

Printed in the United States of America

The paper used in this book complies with the Permanent Paper Standard issued by the National Information Standards Organization (Z39.48-1984).

10 9 8 7 6 5 4 3 2 1

# Contents

# Figures and Tables

## FIGURES



## TABLES

# Preface and Acknowledgments

This book presents a five-year study of Mobiltown. During this period we followed the case of this deprived Israeli town, which attempted to upgrade its status by attracting a large group of new residents from higher social strata and different ethnic origins.

The book represents a joint effort of the three of us. We collaborated in all stages of the study, from its inception through the writing of the final manuscript. Each of us wrote the draft of three out of the nine chapters. Together we revised the entire work. We share equal and collective responsibility for this book, and our names therefore appear in alphabetical order on its cover.

Our work was made possible thanks to the support of many organizations and individuals. A grant from the Ford Foundation through the Israel Foundation Trustees supported the initial stages of our study, including parts of the first population survey of Mobiltown. Additional aspects of the first survey were supported by the Israeli National Council of Research and Development. The council also granted us the means to conduct the second population survey. The Sapir Fund of Mifal-Hapais Foundation and the Pinhas Sapir Center for Development at Tel Aviv University enabled us to carry out the comprehensive data analysis required. The study of the educational system in Mobiltown was made possible by the Research Unit of Sociology of Education and the Community of the School of Education at Tel Aviv University. We are indebted to all these organizations. Without their support this endeavor would not have been possible. The Institute of Social Research in the Department of

Sociology and Anthropology at Tel Aviv University handled the administration of most of the research grants. We thank the institute and particularly its secretary, Ruth Bookstein, for this help.

Several research assistants were most helpful at various stages. Haia Jamshy conducted the collection of data on the education system and the students. Her work for us was preliminary to the development of a Ph.D. thesis on the education system in Mobiltown. Haya Stier and Nitza Berkowitz administered the data collection and analysis of the first population survey. The work of Dafna Kariv and Ricky Melman was instrumental in further stages of the study. The students in the sociology seminar on social policy and social integration collected part of the observational data reported in the book. The help of all these individuals, as well as of Tamar Berkowitz in editing the final manuscript and Alice Zilcha in putting the manuscript into a publishable form, is much appreciated by us.

Above all, we were able to carry out this study thanks to the Mobiltowners themselves. We had enlightening discussions with the mayors of the town and with numerous officials. We benefited from their comments on the study design and from their active participation in the symposium in Mobiltown, where we presented our findings. We would like to thank the nearly 2,000 Mobiltowners, adults and children, for their willing cooperation in the various surveys and observations we conducted.

Hanna Ayalon, Eliezer Ben-Rafael, Abraham Yogev
Tel Aviv University, Israel

1

# The Mobile Community: Status Enhancement, Social Integration, and Neighborhood Differentiation

Urban communities, whether they are large cities or smaller towns, are not fixed social entities. They are in constant flux, due to either general processes of social change or specific projects of planned urban development. This book is about the "settle with us" project in Mobiltown. This is a fictional name of an Israeli town, established in 1949 by Jewish immigrants from North Africa and the Middle East. For three decades it was inhabited mainly by Mizrachim (Jews of Asian-African origin), characterized by low socioeconomic attainments. Only a few of Mobiltown's residents joined the social strata dominated by the ethnocultural group of Ashkenazim (Jews of European-American ancestry).

Toward the end of the 1970s, the political elite of Mobiltown initiated the "settle with us" project. Allocating undeveloped areas to new residential neighborhoods, it offered individual lots for detached and semidetached houses for sale. The project was specifically aimed at attracting new residents of higher socioeconomic strata, Ashkenazim and Mizrachim alike, by offering them a high standard of housing at relatively low expense. Some of the new residents arrived individually; others—especially families of military personnel—came on a group basis. A group of veteran Mobiltowners who could afford it joined the new neighborhoods. By the mid-1980s, the residents of the new neighborhoods amounted to a third of Mobiltown's population.

The "settle with us" project of Mobiltown rested on two grounds. On one hand, it was aimed at enhancing the status of the entire community by attracting new residents of high socioeconomic strata. On the other hand, it used the ideological umbrella of social integration to depict the desired relationship between the new and veteran residents of the town.

Mobiltown thus offers an example of community change, which uniquely combines three factors:

1. a planned enhancement of community status, under the leadership of the local political elite;
2. an unusual experiment of residential integration, in which the newcomers are of a higher status than the veteran town residents; and
3. a counterbalance of community differentiation by new and veteran neighborhoods. Within this planned residential system, specific neighborhoods may turn into status groups, enforcing a distinct community stratification.

Our study evaluates the "settle with us" project on the combined basis of these three factors. It incorporates surveys of new and veteran residents, interviews, and observations, conducted over a period of several years. These enable a comprehensive microlevel analysis of the Mobiltown experiment in community change. In this chapter we explore the theoretical issues involved in this social experiment.

## STATUS ENHANCEMENT OF URBAN COMMUNITIES: MACROLEVEL VERSUS MICROLEVEL ISSUES

### Community Status and Its Enhancement

The status enhancement of Mobiltown was a major calculated aim of the "settle with us" project. American studies of the stratification of urban communities—cities, towns, and suburbs— report some changes in their relative ranking, despite the general tendency of status persistence (Stahura, 1987). Most studies in the United States define a community's status by either the mean (or median) educational level or income level of its inhabitants (Guest, 1978; Logan and Schneider, 1981) or by both coupled with a measure of the residents' average occupational status (Collver and Semyonov, 1979; Stahura, 1987). Hence, improvement in community status actually means growth in the proportion of inhabitants with high socioeconomic characteristics.

Israeli researchers who directly studied the social perceptions of the stratification of communities report that communities are indeed perceived as stratified units. The socioeconomic status of the inhabitants appears to be the central predictor of the prestige assigned to Israeli communities (Semyonov and Kraus, 1982). However, another study on community stratification in Israel (Weintraub and Kraus, 1982) reveals that the stratification of communities by the achieved status of their inhabitants (education, occupation, and income) is congruent with ascribed status attributes (the ethnocultural distribution of the inhabitants and the education and occupation of the inhabitants' fathers).

Due to the interrelations of ethnicity and socioeconomic status and to community variations in opportunity structures, the status of Israeli urban communities rests on both ascription and achievement. Indeed, the only study reporting on status changes of Israeli cities and towns (State of Israel, 1977) is based on an index of "population dependence," combining several ascribed and achieved status measures. Similar to the American studies, this study found that most Israeli communities maintained their relative status ranking during the first half of the 1970s. However, some of them enhanced their status during this period.

## Explanations of Status Enhancement

What explains the status enhancement of urban communities? Several models may provide the explanation of this phenomenon (Logan and Schneider, 1981). The most accepted one, the stratification model, stresses the role of local government in the process (Logan, 1978; Molotch, 1976). Within the framework of this approach, communities are viewed as "political actors which enhance their relative status ranking by controlling the volume, and more importantly, the characteristics of in-migrating populations through zoning policies, tax rates, institutionalized racial discrimination, and other similar means" (Stahura, 1987: 270).

Not all students of community stratification agree in their evaluation of the role of local governments in status enhancement processes and the extent to which their specific interests serve the entire community. Harvey Molotch (1973, 1976) and John Logan and Molotch (1987) view the local community as a "growth machine," which expresses the interests of land-based elites to profit through the intensification of land use. The local government is used to assist in competing with other communities for the achievement of this growth. Hence, the political interests of the local government do not necessarily serve the entire community. They might even negate the interests of most residents, as indicated by the recent increase of local grass-roots antigrowth movements.

However, most macrolevel studies on the stratification of communities are based on the implicit notion that growth and enhancement of community status are desirable for both the local authorities and the local inhabitants. This assumption perhaps stems from Long's (1958) influential depiction of the local community as "an ecology of games." The community, argued Long, consists of a variety of social groups and organizations, each playing its own game of interests. It is the combination of these specific games, motivated by the different interests, that best serves the common interest of the entire community.

This assumption is perhaps appropriate at the macrolevel of analysis, which compares different communities and uses entire communities as units of analysis. The community, taken as a whole, may then benefit from the enhancement of its social status, especially in comparison with other, immobile communities. The picture may appear more complicated at the microlevel of analysis, which concerns the internal processes within an individual community.

## Microlevel Issues of Status Enhancement

At the microlevel, improvement in the status of a specific community primarily means an encounter between lower-status veteran inhabitants and higher-status newcomers. Encounters between various status groups, which differ in their socioeconomic status, ethnicity, or both, carry the seeds of social conflict. However, little is known of the nature of such conflict and its intensity in the setting of an upwardly mobile community. In this respect, the present study constitutes a pioneer attempt to analyze the internal processes within such a community.

The literature on reactions to changes in the social composition of communities seldom deals with the composition pattern described above. In the common pattern, the newcomers are those who constitute the lower-status groups. This pattern usually results from residential desegregation programs, in which minority groups are resettled in more affluent communities or neighborhoods. The focus then is on the reactions of the higher-status veterans to lower-status newcomers. Such reactions are often interpreted as a response to the status threat derived from the proximity to a new, inferior group.

Obviously, this line of reasoning is hardly relevant to the encounter between lower-status veteran residents and higher-status newcomers. In this situation we can trace different sources of social conflict: the long-term residents, or a part of them, may gradually become a marginal group in their community, while the higher-status newcomers may grow into the main holders of social power.

Such a process may involve different reactions of separate groups of residents. First of all, the newcomers may look down at the lower-status veterans, whom they joined because of some personal benefits, and not out of altruism. This may further enhance their self-isolation, self-pride, and determination to use their greater personal resources in order to gain power and control the community.

The veteran inhabitants, though of lower status than the newcomers, may themselves be divided into different social strata. Some of them (the more mobile ones) may join the newcomers. It is unclear what their attitudes would then be toward both the newcomers and the other veteran residents. The majority of the veterans may enjoy the new community status. Their own property value may rise as a result of the status enhancement process. Though they may feel that they are inferior to the newcomers, they may also have more pride in their community in general. However, the poorest group of the veterans may develop resentment toward the newcomers. Comparing themselves with the newcomers, they may feel more deprived than they used to, whether this is anchored in objective reality or not.

These different reactions may enhance the conflicts among various social groups in the mobile community. It is clear that special attention should therefore be given to the social integration of newcomers and veterans. It is not surprising, then, that in planning the "settle with us" project, the political leaders of Mobiltown stressed the ideology of social integration. In doing so, they were probably aware of the possibility that they might lose their political power and leadership positions to the newcomers. But more important, they were aware of the potential community conflicts that were liable to result from the status enhancement project. It is thus important to assess the potential of social integration in an upwardly mobile community, in comparison to more common strategies of social or ethnic integration.

## RESIDENCE AND SOCIAL INTEGRATION: COMMON STRATEGIES VERSUS THE MOBILTOWN MODEL

### Social Conflicts and Residential Segregation

Policies endorsing social integration, in residential settings and otherwise, are the product of two social factors. First, the congruence of ethnic affiliation with socioeconomic status in many Western societies has resulted in ethnic and social class gaps, which have actually created opposing blocks of dominant and subordinate groups. Second, these gaps are the major source of social conflicts between the groups, evidenced in most life areas. Such conflicts find their expression in various social problems, such as alienation, political domination, monopoly over resources and services, negative group self-images and intergroup relations, and social segregation.

Spatial segregation, as well as segregation in various social institutions, constitutes both a major cause and a result of class and ethnic conflicts. An increased awareness of the issue since the 1960s and the development of desegregation policies have brought about a large number of studies on ethnic residential segregation in urban areas. Though most of the work on the topic is American, studies of residential segregation have also spread to other countries, such as Australia (e.g., Jones, 1967), Canada (e.g., Darroch and Marston, 1971; Balakrishnan, 1976, 1982), and Israel (e.g., Klaff, 1973, 1977; Kraus, 1984; Kraus and Koresh, 1992).

American studies from the 1970s on reveal that, despite various desegregation policies and the expectations that the social and economic mobility groups would lessen the ethnic segregation in American urban communities, residential segregation persists and has even increased over the last few decades (Guest and Weed, 1976; Van Valey, Roof, and Wilcox, 1977; Kantrowitz, 1981; Massey, 1985). Perhaps the most notable exception is the case of the suburbs of metropolitan areas, which have undergone extensive growth due to migration out of central cities. American blacks experience significantly less segregation in suburban areas than in the cities. However, Hispanics and Asians are segregated to the same extent in both cities and suburbs (Massey and Denton, 1988).

In Israel too, residential segregation of the major ethnocultural groups, the dominant Ashkenazim and the subordinate Mizrachim, has been a central issue since the mass migration to Israel of Asian-African Jews in the early 1950s. Most of the immigrants in the early statehood years were settled in transit camps, which later became marginal neighborhoods of various cities and towns. Many of them were relocated, under the government policy of population dispersion in the 1950s, to newly built towns named "development towns"; Mobiltown was one of them. They were joined by later immigrants, mostly Mizrachim, in the late 1950s and early 1960s. The concentration of Mizrachim in development towns has restricted their mobility opportunities (Spilerman and Habib, 1976; Semyonov and Tyree, 1981) and has contributed to their ethnocultural identification as Mizrachim, beyond their ethnic identities by specific countries of origin (Ayalon, Ben-Rafael, and Sharot, 1986, 1988).

No wonder, then, that studies on residential segregation in Israeli cities and towns find a persistent pattern of segregation by specific ethnicities or countries of origin (Klaff, 1973, 1977; Kraus, 1984). Especially noticeable is the congruence between residential segregation according to specific ethnicities and segregation according to ethnocultural affiliation: there is more segregation between Ashkenazim and Mizrachim than between specific ethnic groups within each of these two large categories. Ethnic residential segregation is also congruent with criteria of socioeconomic status. However, similar to the situation in the United States, residential segregation in Israel is more widespread in large cities than in the suburbs (Kraus and Koresh, 1992).

## Strategies of Social Integration

Given these structural patterns, views on interethnic relations in Israel range from perspectives of assimilation and cultural pluralism to those of ethnocultural division of labor and internal colonialism (e.g., Ben-Rafael, 1982, 1985; Smooha, 1978, 1984; Swirski, 1981). Regardless of their specific view, researchers recommend some sort of social integration as a remedy to ethnic segregation and conflict.

Various policies of social and ethnic integration have been implemented in Israel, as elsewhere. Here we classify them into three major strategies and briefly discuss the difficulties of each one. Later, we compare these strategies with the unique social integration model of Mobiltown.

### *Indirect Integration*

Under this heading we group the attempts to improve the housing and living conditions of weaker ethnic and socioeconomic groups within their present ecological frameworks. Policies included in this strategy are, for example, slum rehabilitation, neighborhood renewal and self-help projects, welfare programs in education, and the development of special communal services in poor communities. The objective of this strategy is not to promote immediate integration, but rather to reach it ultimately by improving the chances of the lower-status groups to measure up to the others. A major underlying ideology of some of these policies concerns citizens' participation in decisions regarding their own life (Landsberger, 1980; Kweit and Kweit, 1981).

In Israel, the two major policies that follow this strategy are Project Renewal, a 1977 government policy of neighborhood rehabilitation, and the educational welfare program of the Ministry of Education and Culture, which since the 1970s has promoted special education projects for disadvantaged students. Recent evaluations of these policies reveal that their centralized administration resulted in confusion and unclarity regarding the specific aims and activities of both neighborhood rehabilitation (Spiro, 1988) and educational welfare (Yogev, 1989a). Project Renewal, while improving the physical environment of the participating neighborhoods, did not increase the social mobility of their inhabitants (Carmon, 1988). The inhabitants' participation in the project was only partly successful, mainly in terms of local involvement, since the decentralized activities were subordinated to a rather centralized decision-making process (Churchman, 1987; Alterman and Hill, 1988).

These evaluations reflect the two major difficulties of the general strategy. First, the planning and execution of the various welfare programs are usually carried out under the auspices and supervision of the central political establishment, making local participation and cooperation more difficult. The strategy also increases the dependence of the weaker groups on central political institutions, while this dependence is in itself one of the obstacles to integration. The second problem is the essential contradiction between the stated aim of integration and the support this strategy lends, de facto, to the continuation of the existing segregation.

*Direct Institutional Integration*

Under this heading we gather all the attempts to integrate directly members of different ethnoclass groups in defined organizational frameworks, such as schools, workplaces, military units, or political organizations. The aim of this strategy is to promote integration through an encounter in a specific area of activity. It is envisaged that such a meeting will influence integration in other life areas.

The most widespread use of this strategy is in the field of education. School desegregation policies have been implemented in the United States and in other countries since the 1970s (St. John, 1975; Stephan and Feagin, 1986; Yogev and Tomlinson, 1989). Their immediate aim was to equalize the educational opportunities of dominant and subordinate ethnic groups. In Israel, too, a policy of school integration between Ashkenazi and Mizrachi students followed the school reform of 1969 (Blass and

Amir, 1984). In contrast to the United States, however, this policy has shifted its focus from the instrumental aim of equal opportunities to an emphasis on the symbolic value of ethnic integration (Yogev, 1989b).

One of the claims of school desegregation policies is that school integration might have, in addition to long-range results, immediate effects on social integration of the adult population. For instance, it has been established in the United States that a desegregated school system weakens ethnic considerations in the choice of housing (Tauber, 1979; Peerce, 1981).

However, this strategy, too, encounters difficulties. First, the intergroup interaction does not necessarily enhance the integration between the mixed groups, even within the restricted institutional setting. This is due to the status inequality of the participants and to the isolation of the situation from the wider segregative reality (Glaser, 1975). Second, it seems to be difficult to prevent the creation of substitute services by the stronger groups, as shown by the White Flight process subsequent to educational desegregation in the United States (Coleman, Kelly, and Moore, 1975).

### *Residential Integration*

The objective of this strategy, in its present form, is to promote comprehensive integration by placing weaker groups in better-off communities or neighborhoods, which are expected to absorb them. The achievements that might be expected in such a case are the transfer of middle-class values to lower classes and subordinate ethnicities; increased aspirations for mobility on the part of the weaker groups; and an increase in their level of involvement and participation in the leadership of the community (Gans, 1961; Sarkisean, 1976).

The major problem this strategy presents is the preservation of the mutual labeling of the various groups as "absorbers" and "absorbees," "strong" and "weak." When based on this labeling, social integration between the groups is prevented by the inequality in status. This is mainly because the newcomers in the community constitute the lower-status group. This has been the pattern of most residential desegregation projects. For instance, various American studies have dealt with black newcomers in white communities (e.g., Berry et al., 1976; Stahura, 1986). The focus of such studies is generally on the reaction of the higher-status veteran inhabitants toward the lower-status newcomers. These reactions vary in their nature and intensity, but they all share resentment and hostility toward the newcomers, whether they are of a subordinate ethnicity or of a lower social class. These reactions are often interpreted as a response to the status threat derived from the proximity of the veteran inhabitants to an inferior group (Gans, 1967; Pettigrew, 1973; Berry et al., 1976).

Similar reactions are reported by Israeli studies evaluating specific experiments of settling lower-status Mizrachim in better-off neighborhoods and communities, mainly inhabited by Ashkenazim (Shuval, 1962; Marans, 1978; Lazerwitz, 1985). Both the American and the Israeli studies point to the possibility that the settling of lower-strata groups in an established neighborhood may lower the status of that neighborhood. Subsequently, many of the veteran inhabitants may leave the neighborhood, thereby restoring the segregative situation.

## The Mobiltown Model of Social Integration

In all three strategies depicted above, two central trends stand out, both making the objective of integration more difficult to reach. First, all the strategies follow an ideology of patronage. Stronger groups, or the central political establishment, are in charge of planning and executing the integrative activity. Thus, all the different activities are anchored in a framework of dependency that, in principle, contrasts with the aim of integration. Second, the strategies of direct integration, both institutional and residential, are based on a melting pot ideology, according to which the weaker group is expected to accept the stronger group as a model. This principle preserves the inequality between the groups and the negative labeling of the weaker group, thus lowering the chances of success.

The integration model of Mobiltown has tried to overcome these two inherent weaknesses. The intention of the "settle with us" project was to move a higher-status group to a community composed mainly of a weak population. The project was the initiative of the local political elite, and not of some centralized political establishment. Furthermore, the stronger group, which in this case joined the weaker veterans, arrived by its own choice and was aware of the integrative objectives of the project. It joined a small urban community, in which many of the public services were a priori organized on an integrative basis.

These features of the local integration model of Mobiltown seemed to ensure, at least in the planning phase of the project, that the integration between the stronger newcomers and the weaker veterans would become a successful reality. The project avoided both problems of the usual population composition of common integration schemes and the dependence on centralized political establishments. It offered, in contrast, the environment of a small, almost intimate urban community, whose leaders were committed to the project's success. It is the combination of these factors that makes Mobiltown's model quite a unique integration. The assessment of the success of this integration scheme is important both practically and in principle. The uniqueness of the Mobiltown model, which is supposed to overcome the usual difficulties of integration projects, may turn this study into a critical test of the entire theory advocating socioecological integration.

## NEIGHBORHOODS AS STATUS GROUPS: FORCES OF COMMUNITY DIFFERENTIATION

Despite the success prospects of the Mobiltown integration model, one cannot preclude the potential influence of social differentiation within the town on reverse trends, such as social segregation and conflict. In particular, we refer to the settlement of the newcomers in their own separate neighborhoods. This was required by the necessary geographical expansion of the town. It also resulted from the wish to attract higher-status newcomers by offering them the opportunity to build their own homes in privileged living conditions. The newcomers arrived either as individual families or in groups (military families) and settled in two separate neighborhoods. In addition, the veteran neighborhoods of Mobiltown differ among themselves as well—some of them are poor and distressed neighborhoods, while others are relatively better-off.

Considering this geoecological picture as a whole, it appears that Mobiltown is composed of a net of neighborhood groups, distinguished from each other by geographical location, standard of living, and length of residence in the town. We should consider the potential effect of this mosaic of neighborhood groups on the relations between the new and veteran residents.

## The Importance of Neighborhoods

The importance of urban neighborhoods in shaping individual behavior and the life of social groups was largely neglected until the 1960s. This is perhaps due to the long-term effects of Louis Wirth's work on urban sociology. Wirth (1938) argued that population density and heterogeneity in the growing cities caused the breakdown of social relationships and organizational frameworks, including the neighborhood. Despite contrasting views (e.g., Park, Burgess, and McKenzie, 1925), Wirth's conception of urban dwellers as atomized and isolated persisted in urban sociology for several decades.

However, from the 1960s on there has been a steadily growing number of studies focused on urban neighborhoods and their effects in various life areas. For example, friendship patterns of American urban residents were found to be constrained by neighborhood affiliation: persons residing in a neighborhood where a particular social class was more dominant were more likely to have friends from that class regardless of their own social class (Huckfeldt, 1983).

Various political scientists have found neighborhood effects on personal support of particular political parties in the United States (e.g., Foladare, 1968; Segal and Wildstrom, 1970; Wright, 1977), Britain (Butler and Stokes, 1974), and Chile (Prysby, 1975). A more recent and comprehensive study of white neighborhoods in Buffalo and Detroit (Huckfeldt, 1986) reveals a contextual effect of the neighborhood on a variety of politics-related orientations and behaviors: partisan and ethnic loyalties, residential satisfaction and White Flight, and political participation. Finally, several studies have demonstrated neighborhood effects on intergroup relations, resulting from either the racial mixture (Orbell and Sherrill, 1969; Wilson, 1971) or the social class composition (Berger, 1960; Gans, 1967) of the neighborhood.

However, many of the quantitative studies on neighborhood influence approach it in terms of "contextual effects." A neighborhood influence is identified whenever the compositional attributes affect attitudes or behaviors beyond the impact of the same individual-level attributes. Thus, in this approach "the neighborhood is of interest as a structural factor in the lives of its residents, rather than as a well-articulated social organization" (Huckfeldt, 1986, p.2). Although it stems from a long-standing tradition in social research (Davis, Spaeth, and Huson, 1961), it seems that the contextual approach avoids direct consideration of the nature of neighborhood effects.

## Neighborhoods as Status Groups

A different approach to neighborhoods, more relevant to our study, is based on their definition as status groups. This term refers to groups that share a common life-style and are thus identified, by themselves and by others, according to their distinct status. The concept stems from Max Weber's (1946) important distinction between the social stratification of status groups and the labor market stratification of social classes. However, sociological studies that use the concept of status groups have applied it mainly to well-defined occupational groups: political, economic, and military elites (Mills, 1956) or professional groups in general (Collins, 1975, 1979).

Since status groups may be defined by their maintenance of exclusionary boundaries (Collins, 1979), the concept may be applied to a variety of groups of people who, through their shared lifestyle, serve as their own gatekeepers. Occupational groups, recreational groups, and neighborhood groups are important examples. Widely interpreted, the concept does not necessarily require that the groups belong to the upper social classes. Groups of low socioeconomic level, such as slum neighborhoods, may also maintain a common life-style (sometimes called "poverty culture") and thus obtain an exclusive status.

Residential neighborhoods, in particular, provide opportunities inductive to the formation of status groups. In urban societies, residence has become a major status symbol, and lifestyles are shaped to a large extent according to where people live (Logan and Molotch, 1987: 99-146). Therefore, urban neighborhoods have become a major marker of status groups and, by that token, a factor shaping their boundaries. Of course, not all urban neighborhoods do so. Some of them are just locales people live in. But since lifestyles are formed within neighborhoods, relatively homogeneous lifestyles may develop in some neighborhoods and subsequently shape the residents as a distinct status group.

The residents' affiliation with the neighborhood status group does not necessarily imply that they form a cohesive community in the sociological sense. Each resident does not necessarily have to know all the other residents or to restrict personal friendship networks to the neighborhood. In fact, this is almost never the case, especially in urban areas. Status group participation in neighborhoods simply implies the sharing of a common lifestyle and the recognition of the distinctive status it provides.

## Neighborhood Groups in Mobiltown

Mobiltown's neighborhoods, especially since the "settle with us" project was launched, do provide the opportunity for the establishment of status groups. First, the newcomers arrived in two groups. The military families arrived on a group basis; the families already knew each other, they were settled together, and the men had a common occupational background. All these factors provide a sufficient basis for a status group formation. The other newcomers arrived individually, but they were settled separately from the military families. They all built luxurious houses. Their outstanding standard of living distinguishes them from the rest of the Mobiltowners. The veterans who joined them in this luxury quarter probably form a status group of their own, since they are distinctively the upwardly mobile veterans.

The veteran neighborhoods include several status groups as well. Their formation, however, is strongly related to their social class conditions. Most notably, the veterans of the poor neighborhoods form a status group distinguished by its distressed position in town and by the fact that their quarters are recognized as rehabilitation neighborhoods. The other veterans, in the better-off neighborhoods, are less easily defined as a status group. Their features as a group may be less crystallized and less intensive than those of other groups. However, these veterans tend to live in similar conditions, usually in condominium apartment buildings, and they share the same commercial, cultural, and recreational services.

It thus appears that the measurement of neighborhood effects in Mobiltown may be best served by dividing the residents into neighborhood groups, using the criteria of geographical location (i.e., ecological neighborhoods) and length of residence in town (i.e., newcomers versus veterans). The effect of neighborhood group affiliation on the attitudes and behaviors of the residents can then be assessed apart from the effect of individual traits. This is not the usual "contextual effect" treatment of neighborhood influence. Our neighborhood groups do not merely differ from each other in a single specific context, such as the socioeconomic composition of their members. Though this difference may exist, their conceptualization as status groups rests on a number of characteristics distinguishing each group from the others. Common military background, luxurious private housing, and poverty subculture are all exclusive status group criteria that distinguish each status group from the others but do not cut across all the neighborhood groups.

It is this formation of neighborhood groups that is most relevant for studying the effects of community differentiation in Mobiltown. Support of the town's integration model and, more importantly, social conflicts and disagreements on critical issues of local life may well be influenced by status group distinctions among the Mobiltowners.

## THE MAJOR QUESTIONS AND OUTLINE OF THE STUDY

As this chapter shows, our approach to Mobiltown rests on three theoretical conceptualizations: the status enhancement of an upwardly mobile community; the social integration model it attempted to implement by the "settle with us" project; and the establishment of neighborhood groups as distinct status groups, following the arrival of the newcomers.

In accordance with these theoretical approaches we can now pose three major sets of questions that our study attempts to answer:

1. How does the status enhancement project affect the internal stratification of Mobiltown? What kind of new residents does such a project attract, and what are their motivations to settle down in a town known for its low prestige? To what extent does their arrival influence the entire local stratification system, considering all the groups of new and veteran residents?
2. To what extent can such a project achieve the implementation of social integration among new and

veteran residents? Was the aim of social integration achieved in everyday life patterns and lifestyles, in the self-perceptions and intergroup attitudes of each residential group, and in their perceptions of Mobiltown's local politics and political future? An answer to these questions may illuminate the significance of the attempted integration model, as opposed to the more common strategies of social integration.

3. Does the formation of neighborhood groups, as distinct status groups, affect the life of the Mobiltowners? To what extent does neighborhood group affiliation, beyond individual traits, influence the residents' behaviors, attitudes, and perceptions in various life areas? Are social conflicts among the neighborhood groups traceable, and do they hinder the implementation of social integration?

Following a description of the setting and the study design in chapter 2, each chapter is devoted to a particular question or analyzes a specific life area in view of the questions posed. Chapter 3 provides the social profiles of the neighborhood groups, as well as profiles of migration to Mobiltown by the newcomers. In chapter 4 we discuss the lifestyles and friendship networks of the different groups. The self-perceptions of the neighborhood groups and the way they view each other are discussed in chapter 5, while chapter 6 is devoted to political life in Mobiltown. The children of the new and veteran Mobiltowners and the way they view school integration in town are the foci of chapter 7. Chapter 8 incorporates data collected four years after our initial encounter with the Mobiltowners. It concerns the changes that have occurred during this period in relation to the lifestyles, perceptions, and attitudes of the various neighborhood groups. The conclusion, in chapter 9, attempts to answer the above three sets of questions in view of the preceding empirical analysis.

# 2

# The Setting and the Study Design

## GETTING TO KNOW MOBILTOWN

### The Early Period

Mobiltown was founded in 1949, right after the establishment of the state of Israel. It is located south of metropolitan Tel Aviv. Established as a development town, Mobiltown was considered as such from the time of its foundation until its recent status enhancement. The characteristics of development towns locate them at the bottom of the prestige hierarchy of settlements in Israel (Semyonov and Kraus, 1982). Most development towns were established during the 1950s, away from the populated urban centers. Their settlers were mostly new immigrants from the Middle East or North Africa who were sent there by the settling institutions. The image of the development towns is associated with poverty, unemployment, and restricted educational and occupational opportunities (Spilerman and Habib, 1976). Due to these deficiencies, the migration balance of most development towns is negative, characterized by an out-migration selection—the more successful inhabitants tend to move to better established settlements (Gabriel, Justman, & Levy, 1986).

Similar to most development towns, the majority of Mobiltown's population (over 90 percent) was either of North

African (mainly Moroccan) or Middle Eastern origin (according to the 1972 census). The social profile of its inhabitants fitted the image of a development town: in 1972 about one-third of Mobiltown's population had less than five years of schooling (compared with 13.6 percent among the total Israeli adult Jewish population). The welfare agency supported 43.5 percent of Mobiltown's families (compared with a national figure of 17.5 percent). Most of its working inhabitants (63 percent) were industry workers (compared with 30 percent). Mobiltown differs from most development towns regarding its location—it is quite close to the populated center of Israel. This advantage probably contributed to its ability to launch the "settle with us" project.

### The Shift in Political Power

The recent changes in Mobiltown are rooted in the political shift that took place there in 1974. Until that period, the local council had been headed either by MAPAI (the Labor party), then the largest party in Israel, or by MAFDAL, the National Religious party. The central extended families of Mobiltown, most of them of Moroccan origin, were deeply involved in local politics, and their interests largely influenced the operation of the local authorities, which perpetuated social stagnation. This state of affairs encouraged the organization of "the youngsters," a rebellious group among the first cohorts of high school graduates in town. In its first stages the organization was not affiliated with any political party, and its declared purpose was to change the social climate and the quality of life in town. After a disappointing period as independent delegates in the local council, where they did not achieve significant influence, "the youngsters" joined the local branch LIKUD—then the main opposition party in Israel. They later took this branch over from within and won the 1973 local elections on its ticket. They have headed the local council ever since.

The political shift and the actions of "the youngsters" had an immediate effect on Mobiltown in various areas—housing, education, infrastructure. However, the main contribution of the new authorities to the tremendous change in Mobiltown was the initiation of the "settle with us" project in the late 1970s.

### The "Settle with Us" Project

The "settle with us" project of Mobiltown was launched within the general framework of the Bneh Beitcha (literally, "build your home") project in Israeli development towns. Such projects are generally aimed at raising the living standard of the local residents, by allotting land for private houses at low prices (Efrat, 1987: 159-164). In contrast, Mobiltown's "settle with us" project was initiated with the aim of enhancing the status of the community via improvement of its socioeconomic level. Consequently, its main intention was to attract new residents with higher socioeconomic characteristics. The characteristics of the target population were clearly specified by the planners of the project. The statistical means of the original population of Mobiltown in terms of years of schooling were precisely calculated as an indicator of the population's social status. The characteristics of the target population were defined by the planners according to the gap between the national means and those of the Mobiltowners. The newcomers were expected to close that gap and bring the local averages up to the national means.

"The desired addition of inhabitants: 5250 persons which constitutes 25% of the present population....One question arises at this point—is the addition of 5250 inhabitants indeed necessary?...The educational level of the younger generation [in Mobiltown] is higher than that of the adults. Hence they are expected to improve the relative position of the settlement...it may therefore be assumed that a smaller number of new settlers may produce the desired change... .We are speaking of attracting 3600-4000 persons (75% of 5250) aged 20+ with at least 9 years of schooling. Assuming that we are interested in young families, and assuming that the educational level of both spouses is similar, we speak of 2000 new families with the following distribution: 42% with 9 to 12 years of schooling; 33% with 13 to 15 years; and 25% with 16 and more. Obviously, the inclusion of families with low educational levels must be avoided." (Stoup, 1983: 18-19)

According to the planners, the educational level of the target population ensured an improvement in its two obvious correlates—income and occupational prestige. However, it also ensured a change in the ethnic composition of the town. Since educational level and ethnic origin are highly correlated in Israel, it implies a massive increase in the number of settlers with European-American origin. However, neither the political planners of the "settle with us" project nor their professional advisers had the intention of directly supervising the composition of the forthcoming settlers to assure the desired distribution. The specification of the desired demographic characteristics served the planners in their formulation of the residential preferences of that population in an effort to enhance the attractiveness of Mobiltown.

The attraction of the higher-status population to the unattractive town was not an easy task. The authorities had to provide incentives powerful enough to suppress the negative image of the town. One advantage of the town was its geographic location. As noted, it is not far from the Tel Aviv metropolitan area, which ensures occupational opportunities as well as proximity to the commercial and cultural centers of the country. Consequently, the planners were not very preoccupied with providing occupational opportunities for the potential newcomers (Sliefer and Stoup, 1981). They were concerned, however, with the occupational opportunities available for the female labor force (in their terms, the secondary supporters), since women are less willing to commute. The planned expansion of the education system was perceived as a partial solution to the problem pertaining to this sector of the labor force.

The incentives provided by the authorities were twofold—economic and social. The economic advantage was the low price of the land offered to potential settlers. The social incentive was based on the assumption of the project's social advisers that it would be easier to attract groups of similar families who would like to share the same neighborhood. Based on this assumption and backed by the army, Mobiltown offered a newly established neighborhood (planned for 1,000 detached and semidetached houses) to army officers. Many families of this category joined the military neighborhood on a group basis. Civilian settlers were offered an additional new neighborhood designed for deluxe self-construction. Four hundred such houses were built.

## Mobiltown's Neighborhoods

The "settle with us" project added two neighborhoods to Mobiltown, which was already composed of several very well defined geographic quarters. Prior to the project, Mobiltown was composed of two poor neighborhoods (which we will call Poortown), consisting of about 1,400 families, and three lower-middle-class neighborhoods (hereafter, Midtown), numbering about 3,500 families. Poortown was characterized by both low-standard housing and a disadvantaged population. The rehabilitation of Poortown within the Israeli Project Renewal was part of the planned change of Mobiltown. This included improvement of the physical appearance of buildings and the construction of additional dwelling units for the absorption of new settlers. Midtown was composed of moderate-level housing, both apartment buildings and private houses, and lower-middle-class inhabitants. In the framework of the plans for Mobiltown's expansion, additional apartment buildings were designed for Midtown.

The location of the two new neighborhoods, which are situated in the same area (Newtown), actually segregates them from the veteran neighborhoods of the settlement (Oldtown), with relative proximity to one of the poor neighborhoods. However, in spite of the centrality of the status enhancement of Mobiltown in the design of the project, its planners did consider social integration between the newcomers and the long-term residents as essential. The implementation of social integration was defined as the task of the education system and the commercial and cultural centers.

The creation of a link between Oldtown and Newtown relied on Oldtowners who were expected to move to Newtown. According to the expansion plans, one-third of the land of the new civilian quarter was assigned to veteran inhabitants.

According to the plan for its renewal, Mobiltown was supposed to grow by about 2,500 families (1,000 in Newtown and the rest in Oldtown) during a five-year period (1980-1985). The settling of Newtown started in 1980 and was nearly accomplished by 1983, when the population of Mobiltown had grown by one-third (to about 19,000 residents). This expansion was due to: (1) the "settle with us" project in Newtown, (2) the new settlers in Poortown, and (3) the new settlers in Midtown. Life in a town experiencing notable growth, combined with the enhancement of its status, as well as characteristics and consequences of the encounter between its various social groups, constitutes the central focus of our study.

## THE STUDY DESIGN AND RESEARCH METHODS

### Study Design

The study is based on several data sources: population surveys (of both adult residents and school students), interviews with public officials, and figures and observations of various community activities, for the period between the beginning of 1984 and the end of 1988. The major data source is a survey conducted in 1985. The sampling for this survey is based on six neighborhoods—the military, the new civilian, both poor neighborhoods, and two of the three Midtown quarters (the third is much less populated).

The original design was randomly to sample 100 households in each neighborhood, which would yield 600 interviewees. We decided to include equal samples of the various neighborhoods despite their size differences, since the neighborhoods as units constitute the focus of our research. We are thus interested in a stratified sample of Mobiltown's neighborhoods, not in a representative sample of Mobiltown as a whole. In the neighborhoods composed of both veteran residents and newcomers (the new civilian neighborhood, Midtown, and Poortown), an additional sampling was performed to include 50 of each category. The cutoff year distinguishing newcomers from long-term residents is 1980, the period of the initial settlement of Newtown. Due to the small number of newcomers in both Midtown and Poortown, we were unable to sample 50 new residents. Hence, the final sample includes only 576 respondents. The last phase of the sampling was based on gender—each neighborhood subsample is composed of equal numbers of men and women, representing different households. Interviewees were asked to provide information on their spouses.

The unit of analysis is the neighborhood group—a combination of neighborhood and length of residence. The neighborhood groups that serve as the units of the analyses are: the military quarter (MILIT); newcomers in the new civilian quarter (CIVILNEW); long-term residents in the new civilian quarter (CIVILVET); newcomers in Midtown (MIDNEW); long-term residents in Midtown (MIDVET); newcomers in Poortown (POORNEW); and veterans in Poortown (POORVET).

The survey is based on an interview schedule composed of both closed and open-ended items. The respondents were interviewed in their homes by trained interviewers. The interview schedule concerns a variety of topics related to life in the changing community: attraction to, and satisfaction with, life in Mobiltown; patterns of commercial and cultural consumption; self-perceptions and mutual perceptions of the various neighborhood groups; perceptions of the local political system; and information on friendship networks. In addition, the interview provides information on the socioeconomic and ethnic characteristics of the respondents.

Four years after the first survey, in 1988, we conducted a followup survey. Its main purpose was to tap changes that might have occurred during the four-year period. Details on the second sample are presented in chapter 8, which compares the two periods. The sample sizes of the different neighborhood groups are presented in Table 2.1.

**Table 2.1**
**Distribution of Sample According to Neighborhood Group**

| | First Survey | | Followup Survey | |
|---|---|---|---|---|
| Neighborhood Group | N | % | N | % |
| MILIT | 100 | 17.4 | 78 | 13.7 |
| CIVILNEW | 50 | 8.7 | 112 | 19.7 |
| CIVILVET | 47 | 8.2 | 37 | 6.5 |
| MIDNEW | 75 | 13.1 | 73 | 12.8 |
| MIDVET | 105 | 17.9 | 94 | 16.5 |
| POORNEW | 39 | 6.8 | 39 | 6.9 |
| POORVET | 160 | 27.9 | 136 | 23.9 |
| TOTAL | 576 | 100.0 | 569 | 100.0 |

Alongside the surveys concentrating on the adult population, we conducted several surveys among students at three educational levels—the last year of elementary school (sixth grade), junior high school (seventh to ninth grades), and high school. Details on these surveys are presented in chapter 7, which concentrates on the educational system of Mobiltown.

In order to understand better the processes occurring in Mobiltown, we observed various activities and conducted numerous interviews with central figures in Mobiltown, such as political leaders, social town planners, managers of the welfare agency, organizers of cultural activities, and other Mobiltowners. Their advice was also important and useful for the construction of the interview schedule.

## Methods of Analysis

In addition to a descriptive analysis, which depicts the differences among the various neighborhood groups, multivariate analysis was based on two methods—discriminant analysis and the linear structural relation model. Discriminant analysis is used for the construction of profiles of the neighborhood groups in terms of various aspects of life in Mobiltown (lifestyles, friendship networks, perceptions). The linear structural relation model serves decomposition and separation of the net effect of the neighborhood group from that of the residents' socioeconomic characteristics in the formation of behaviors and attitudes. In these analyses the neighborhood groups are treated as distinct constructs (dummy variable combinations of neighborhood group affiliations). This differs from the regular contextual effect treatment of neighborhoods, which rests on the compositional attributes of individual residents. In accordance with our theoretical point of departure, this treatment assumes that the neighborhood groups are status groups whose significance surpasses that of contextual composition. Further details on the two methods appear in the appendix.

# 3

# The Mobiltowners: New and Veteran Neighborhood Groups

Our point of departure is the division of Mobiltown into seven neighborhood groups, defined by the combination of two criteria: geographical location and length of residence in town. In this chapter we analyze the social structure of the seven groups, in order to answer some preliminary theoretical questions. First, to what extent did the "settle with us" project result in the status enhancement of Mobiltown, as projected by its planners? This question is answered by comparing the socioeconomic characteristics of the new and veteran neighborhoods.

Second, our analysis aims at exploring the extent to which the seven neighborhood groups may be considered distinct status groups. We may consider them as such if each of the seven has specific social features, above and beyond the general veteran-newcomer distinctions. Referring to this issue, we first analyze the sociodemographic profiles of the seven neighborhood groups. Then, concentrating on the four neighborhood groups of newcomers, we attempt to build profiles of their particular motivations for settling in Mobiltown.

If indeed, the various neighborhood groups appear to have unique profiles in terms of their residents' status, demographic characteristics, and reasons for migrating to Mobiltown, then the chances are high that they will establish themselves as exclusive status groups. As explained in chapter 1, this may well affect the relations between the neighborhood groups and their potential for social integration versus developing intergroup conflicts.

## SOCIODEMOGRAPHIC PROFILES OF THE NEIGHBORHOOD GROUPS

We start by describing separate sociodemographic indicators of the neighborhood groups: their age distribution, ethnic and religious identities, status characteristics, and some indicators of the intergenerational mobility of their residents. Then we attempt to build a sociodemographic profile of the groups from the combination of these separate indicators.

### Age Distribution

Table 3.1 shows the age distribution of all the survey respondents and of the respondents from each neighborhood group. It is clearly noticeable that Mobiltown is a young

**Table 3.1**
**Age Distribution of the New and Veteran Neighborhoods**

| | Mean Age | S.D. |
|---|---|---|
| **Newtown** | | |
| MILIT | 33.9 | 4.2 |
| CIVILNEW | 36.0 | 5.5 |
| CIVILVET | 35.4 | 5.9 |
| **Oldtown** | | |
| MIDNEW | 29.5 | 5.4 |
| MIDVET | 37.1 | 11.7 |
| POORNEW | 29.2 | 6.3 |
| POORVET | 34.0 | 11.6 |
| Total (N=559)* | 33.9 | 9.1 |

* The N in this table, and in all other tables of chapters 3 through 7, refers to the 576 respondents of the first community survey after excluding those with missing information. Computations for each table were based on the presented N.

community: its average adult resident is 34 years old, and the majority of residents are within the range of nine years above or below this mean age. This age distribution may well result from the fact that Mobiltown is a development town rather than a veteran community of the prestate period, and its initial inhabitants were Mizrachim characterized by a high birthrate. Nevertheless, the young mean age of the residents in general may also explain their drive for status enhancement of their community—a drive that might be considered inconceivable in older and more established communities.

As the separate age distributions of the neighborhood groups show, the two youngest groups are the newcomers in Midtown and Poortown. Their young mean age indicates that the two groups are mainly comprised of young families who could not afford the more expensive housing of Newtown. The newcomers in Newtown are somewhat older, in their thirties, and are thus comprised of residents in the middle of their occupational careers. This is true of both CIVILNEW and MILIT, though the mean age of the latter is slightly lower, corresponding to the younger age of military officers.

It is interesting to note that the age distribution of the veteran residents who moved to Newtown is very similar to that of the newcomers in the new civilian neighborhood. This similarity indicates that these two neighborhood groups may have some common features and that CIVILVET may constitute a group of mobile veteran residents. This notion is enhanced by comparing the age distribution of CIVILVET with the distributions of the two veteran groups who remained in Oldtown—MIDVET and POORVET. The age variation of these two groups is wide, showing that the veteran neighborhoods are less homogeneous in age, and consist of older and younger generations (the proportion of young adults in POORVET is larger, as indicated by its mean age). Since it is most likely that CIVILVET originated from MIDVET rather than POORVET, it appears that they constitute a rather specific and homogeneous group of the heterogeneous Midtown veterans—midcareer adults who could afford to build a house in the new project and thus ensure their mobility by joining the Newtown residents.

## Ethnic and Religious Identities

The ethnic and religious identities of the neighborhood groups are presented in Table 3.2. By the term *ethnicity* we refer in this case to the ethnocultural division of Ashkenazim and Mizrachim. Since religiosity and ethnic identity are interrelated in Israel (Mizrachi Jews tend to practice religion more than Ashkenazim do), we add the religious identity of the residents to the present discussion.

The ethnocultural affiliation of the respondents was measured by two indicators: the birth countries of the respondents' paternal grandfathers and those of the respondents themselves. The countries were grouped by three categories: Israel, Asian-African countries, and European-American ones. These two indicators allow us to assess not only the ancestry of the respondents, but also their identity as first or second generations in Israel.

As shown in the first part of Table 3.2, the great majority of the veteran residents of Midtown and Poortown are of Mizrachi ancestry. This is true to an even larger extent with respect to the veteran residents who moved into Newtown. The neighborhood groups of newcomers are more heterogeneous with respect to ethnocultural affiliation. While the majority of newcomers in Oldtown (i.e., MIDNEW and POORNEW) are of Mizrachi ancestry, the majority of newcomers in Newtown (MILIT and CIVILNEW) are Ashkenazim. Yet, there are still many residents of the opposite ethnocultural affiliation in each of these new neighborhood groups. The ethnic heterogeneity of the new groups is further emphasized by the respondents' birthplaces, presented in the second part of the table. In all neighborhood groups of the newcomers, the majority of the residents were born in Israel.

We should note, however, that the group with the highest proportion of first-generation Mizrachim is the veterans in the new civilian neighborhood. This appears to be a particular

**Table 3.2**
**Ethnic and Religious Profiles of the New and Veteran Neighborhoods**

| | MILIT | CIVILNEW | CIVILVET | MIDNEW | MIDVET | POORNEW | POORVET |
|---|---|---|---|---|---|---|---|
| (a) Grandfather's Birthplace | | | | | | | |
| Israel | 6.1 | 6.0 | 0 | 4.0 | 1.0 | 2.6 | 0 |
| Asia-Africa | 22.2 | 36.0 | 97.9 | 64.0 | 82.5 | 74.4 | 89.9 |
| Europe-America | 71.7 | 58.0 | 2.1 | 32.0 | 16.5 | 23.1 | 10.1 |
| Total (N = 571) | 100.0% | 100.0% | 100.0% | 100.0% | 100.0% | 100.0% | 100.0% |
| (b) Respondent's Birthplace | | | | | | | |
| Israel | 66.0 | 50.0 | 27.7 | 57.3 | 38.8 | 76.9 | 35.0 |
| Asia-Africa | 14.0 | 20.0 | 68.1 | 24.0 | 50.5 | 20.5 | 58.1 |
| Europe-America | 20.0 | 30.0 | 4.3 | 18.7 | 10.7 | 2.6 | 6.9 |
| Total (N = 571) | 100.0% | 100.0% | 100.0% | 100.0% | 100.0% | 100.0% | 100.0% |
| (c) Religious Self-Identity | | | | | | | |
| Religious | 1.0 | 2.0 | 21.3 | 13.9 | 21.4 | 12.8 | 25.0 |
| Traditional | 19.0 | 26.0 | 68.1 | 45.8 | 57.3 | 53.8 | 51.9 |
| Free | 31.0 | 36.0 | 4.3 | 22.2 | 18.4 | 23.1 | 18.1 |
| Secular | 49.0 | 36.0 | 6.4 | 18.1 | 2.9 | 10.3 | 5.0 |
| Total (N = 571) | 100.0% | 100.0% | 100.0% | 100.0% | 100.0% | 100.0% | 100.0% |

**Table 3.3**
**Status Characteristics of the New and Veteran Neighborhoods**

| | MILIT | CIVILNEW | CIVILVET | MIDNEW | MIDVET | POORNEW | POORVET |
|---|---|---|---|---|---|---|---|
| (a) Years of Schooling | | | | | | | |
| (Respondents & Spouses; N=545) | | | | | | | |
| Mean | 14.5 | 13.4 | 11.1 | 11.9 | 10.3 | 10.8 | 9.4 |
| S.D. | 2.3 | 2.8 | 2.9 | 2.4 | 3.1 | 2.4 | 3.1 |
| (b) Years of Schooling-Women | | | | | | | |
| (Respondents & Spouses; N=530) | | | | | | | |
| Mean | 13.8 | 12.9 | 11.0 | 11.0 | 10.1 | 10.6 | 8.8 |
| S.D. | 2.3 | 3.1 | 2.9 | 2.0 | 3.2 | 2.1 | 3.5 |
| (c) Occupational Prestige-Men | | | | | | | |
| (Respondents & Spouses; N=474) | | | | | | | |
| Mean | 81.3 | 72.1 | 54.2 | 50.2 | 44.4 | 45.0 | 37.7 |
| S.D. | 15.4 | 25.6 | 20.1 | 21.4 | 21.4 | 19.7 | 17.7 |
| (d) Occupational Prestige-Women | | | | | | | |
| (Respondents & Spouses; N=433) | | | | | | | |
| Mean | 59.1 | 56.8 | 37.7 | 47.7 | 32.2 | 30.4 | 25.3 |
| S.D. | 27.0 | 28.6 | 27.5 | 28.0 | 27.3 | 20.6 | 22.3 |

**Table 3.3 (continued)**

| | MILIT | CIVILNEW | CIVILVET | MIDNEW | MIDVET | POORNEW | POORVET |
|---|---|---|---|---|---|---|---|
| (e) Occupational Class-Men | | | | | | | |
| (Respondents & Spouses; N=517) | | | | | | | |
| Employee | 29.9 | 23.9 | 26.7 | 61.4 | 50.5 | 61.1 | 68.2 |
| Employee-Manager | 65.0 | 39.1 | 33.4 | 30.0 | 29.7 | 11.1 | 18.2 |
| Self-Employed | 5.2 | 17.4 | 15.6 | 4.3 | 9.9 | 16.7 | 6.8 |
| Self-Employed-Manager | .0 | 15.2 | 22.1 | .0 | 3.3 | 8.4 | 0.8 |
| Other (student, pensioner) | .0 | 4.3 | 2.2 | 4.3 | 6.6 | 2.8 | 6.1 |
| Total* | 100.0% | 100.0% | 100.0% | 100.0% | 100.0% | 100.0% | 100.0% |
| (f) Occupational Class - Women | | | | | | | |
| (Respondents & Spouses; N=518) | | | | | | | |
| Employee | 48.5 | 40.8 | 30.4 | 43.9 | 30.9 | 28.2 | 39.0 |
| Employee-Manager | 13.4 | 12.2 | 6.5 | 4.5 | 8.6 | .0 | 6.9 |
| Self-Employed | 3.1 | 10.2 | 4.3 | 1.5 | 2.1 | .0 | 2.9 |
| Self-Employed-Manager | .0 | .0 | 4.3 | .0 | .0 | .0 | 0.4 |
| Other (including housewife) | 35.1 | 36.7 | 54.3 | 48.2 | 58.5 | 71.8 | 50.6 |
| Total* | 100.0% | 100.0% | 100.0% | 100.0% | 100.0% | 100.0% | 100.0% |

* In some cases the total is approximately 100% due to rounding errors.

mobile group of young Mizrachi immigrants, and its ethnic profile stands out in contrast to that of the newcomers in Newtown. This contrast is further accentuated by differences in religious practice.

Religiosity was measured by asking the respondents to identify themselves as "religious" (practicing all religious laws), "traditional" (practicing part of the religious laws), "free" (practicing some religious laws), or "secular" (not practicing religion or opposed to religion). As shown in the third part of Table 3.2, the majority of the Oldtowners identify themselves as religious or traditional, in accordance with their Mizrachi origin. The newcomers of Newtown tend to be secular. The most religious group in Newtown is the veterans. This is not surprising, given the ethnic affiliation of CIVILVET. Yet, it shows that the ethnic and religious composition of this mobile group is quite different from that of its new neighbors and that the civilian neighborhood can in no way be considered homogeneous.

## Status and Mobility Characteristics

The differences among the seven neighborhood groups are further emphasized when we consider more specifically the status characteristics of their residents. Table 3.3 provides information on the educational and occupational levels of the residents of each neighborhood group. Since education and occupation may vary by gender, we combined the data available on the respondents and their spouses and present each gender separately.

Considering education first, it appears that the two groups with the highest schooling for both men and women are the newcomer groups of Newtown—MILIT and CIVILNEW. Below them are the mobile veterans and the new groups of Oldtown, MIDNEW and POORNEW. The veterans of Oldtown, particularly those of Poortown, have attained the lowest average level of education.

The hierarchy is only slightly different regarding occupational prestige. This status indicator was measured by Hartman's

(1979) 100-point scale of Israeli occupational prestige. Since the military ranks of MILIT were not included in the original scale, we assigned each rank the prestige score of the civilian managerial position closest to it in terms of responsibilities and number of subordinate workers.

As the mean prestige scores for men show, the two groups with the highest occupational status are again MILIT and CIVILNEW. The very high mean prestige score of MILIT reflects the high military ranks of its males (38 percent of them hold the rank of lieutenant colonel or higher). The mean prestige score of CIVILVET, though third in descending order, is far below that of these two groups and resembles that of MIDNEW. Next in descending order are POORNEW and MIDVET, while the Poortown veterans attain the lowest mean prestige score. The picture is very similar with respect to the occupational prestige of women, with the exception of the somewhat lower than expected score of the CIVILVET women.

Thus, in contrast to the nondefinite ethnocultural divisions between new and veteran residents in Mobiltown, a clear status hierarchy has been established: the newcomers of Newtown are at the top, the other newcomers—especially in Midtown—and the Newtown veterans are in the middle, and the Oldtown veterans—especially those in Poortown—are at the bottom of the hierarchy.

The veterans in the new civilian neighborhood, though constituting a mobile group relative to the other veterans, fall far below the newcomers of Newtown in terms of educational and occupational attainments. However, in one aspect of status they do resemble the newcomers in the civilian neighborhood. The last two parts of Table 3.3 classify the men and women of each neighborhood by occupational class. This classification is based primarily on the categories of employees versus self-employed. Each of these categories is further divided into nonmanagerial versus managerial positions (i.e., whether the respondent is in charge of other workers).

As the occupational classification of the men shows, there is a clear-cut division between Oldtown and Newtown. The modal category for all Oldtown groups, regardless of length of residence in Mobiltown, is that of nonmanagerial employees. In the two Midtown neighborhoods an additional large proportion of the men are occupied in managerial employee positions. In Newtown, there is a wide difference between the military and civilian neighborhoods. While the majority of MILIT are managerial employees, in accordance with their military positions, the CIVILNEW and CIVILVET men present a very similar distribution of occupational classes. In both groups the majority are still employees, especially in managerial positions. Yet, a large portion of the men in both groups—33 percent of the men in CIVILNEW and 38 percent in CIVILVET—are self-employed.

This shows that there are some points of resemblance between the newcomers and veterans of the new civilian neighborhood, despite their differences in levels of status attainment. CIVILVET represents a very specific mobile group, which through self-employment has attained economic mobility. Despite their economic success, these mobile veterans do not resemble CIVILNEW in their educational attainment or occupational prestige, though they rank higher in these respects than other veterans. In some respects, such as ethnic and religious identities and the high proportion of nonworking women (see the last part of Table 3.3), they are still most similar to the Midtown veterans of whom they were originally a part.

These last points are further demonstrated by a comparison of the status of origin and some intergenerational mobility patterns of the neighborhood groups. These analyses should be approached cautiously, since the parents of most of the residents, both newcomers and veterans, were immigrants who came from countries with different stratification systems and experienced a shift in occupational career upon arrival. As shown in Table 3.4, CIVILVET, similar to all other Oldtown groups, originated from lower-status families, as indicated by their fathers' education and occupational prestige. The newcomers of Newtown, in both military and civilian neighborhoods, come from families of significantly higher status. These different origins created different patterns of intergenerational mobility.

**Table 3.4**
**Status of Origin and Intergenerational Mobility by Neighborhood Groups**

| | MILIT | CIVILNEW | CIVILVET | MIDNEW | MIDVET | POORNEW | POORVET |
|---|---|---|---|---|---|---|---|
| (a) Percentage of fathers with postsecondary education (N=557) | 15.3 | 29.2 | 0 | 4.0 | 3.0 | 2.6 | 1.9 |
| (b) Father's occupational prestige (N=462) | | | | | | | |
| Mean | 54.2 | 52.8 | 38.3 | 40.6 | 38.7 | 35.8 | 36.6 |
| S.D. | 23.2 | 23.3 | 20.1 | 23.3 | 21.4 | 23.3 | 18.9 |
| (c) Percentage of respondents (R) whose level of schooling is higher than that of their fathers (F),by gender (N=557) | | | | | | | |
| **Men** | | | | | | | |
| R-secondary, F-primary | 1.1 | 16.7 | 25.0 | 17.3 | 13.0 | 25.6 | 23.3 |
| R-postsecondary;F-secondary or primary | 29.3 | 14.6 | 6.8 | 13.3 | 6.0 | .0 | 3.1 |
| **Women** | | | | | | | |
| R-secondary, F-primary | 5.4 | 10.4 | 18.2 | 21.3 | 23.0 | 0.6 | 15.1 |
| R-postsecondary;F-secondary or primary | 21.7 | 10.4 | 15.9 | 8.0 | 3.0 | 2.6 | 2.5 |

Using the indicator of educational mobility, we can see from the last part of Table 3.4 that the male newcomers of Newtown obtained intergenerational mobility mainly by the attainment of higher education. The CIVILVET men may be considered educationally mobile mainly in the sense of possessing secondary schooling; in this respect they resemble the Poortown residents. However, by using their education for advancing their own business ventures, rather than joining the sector of employees, they have secured their economic mobility.

The picture is somewhat different for the CIVILVET women, who either are employees or have chosen to remain housewives. Compared with the other veterans, they tend to become educationally mobile, relative to their fathers, by attaining postsecondary or higher education. In this feature they resemble the other Newtown women, rather than the Oldtowners.

## A Profile of the Neighborhood Groups

Up to this point we have discussed separate sociodemographic indicators of the neighborhood groups, thereby revealing an intricate net of resemblances and differences among the seven groups. But is it possible to build a sociodemographic profile of the neighborhood groups out of all these indicators put together?

In order to answer this question, we performed a multivariate discriminant analysis, in which the seven neighborhood groups were discriminated by a list of eight indicators: ethnocultural affiliation, generation in Israel, age, religiosity, years of schooling, intergenerational mobility in education, occupational prestige, and occupational class (employees versus self-employed). Table 3.5, presenting the results of the analysis, shows the three statistically significant functions of discrimination that emerged, in order of discriminant power.

The first function holds the strongest discriminant power (as indicated by the high canonical correlation and the low Wilks' Lambda coefficient). As shown by the group centroids (which are the mean function scores of each neighborhood group), this first function differentiates between the newcomers of Newtown

(MILIT and CIVILNEW, both with high positive scores) and the rest of the neighborhood groups, which have negative function scores. The highest mean negative score is that of POORVET.

**Table 3.5**
**Discriminant Analysis: Sociodemographic Characteristics of the Neighborhood Groups (N=446)**

| Discriminating Variables and Standardized Discriminant Coefficients | Function 1 | Function 2 | Function 3 |
|---|---|---|---|
| Grandfather's birth continent: Asia-Africa* | -.34 | .25 | .10 |
| Respondent's birth country: Israel* | .18 | -.03 | -.37 |
| Age | .28 | .71 | .33 |
| Religiosity (1=secular ... 4= religious) | -.38 | .29 | .02 |
| Years of schooling | .33 | .30 | -.28 |
| Educational mobility** | -.09 | .34 | -.25 |
| Occupational prestige | .49 | .19 | .35 |
| Occupational class: employees (incl. managers)* | -.10 | -.63 | .55 |
| Canonical correlation | .75 | .36 | .24 |
| Wilks' Lambda | .34 | .77 | .89 |
| p ($x^2$ test) | <.001 | <.001 | .001 |
| **Group Centroids** | | | |
| MILIT | 1.77 | -.19 | .11 |
| CIVILNEW | 1.40 | .36 | -.05 |
| CIVILVET | -.61 | .83 | .08 |
| MIDNEW | -.25 | -.28 | -.25 |
| MIDVET | -.64 | .43 | .01 |
| POORNEW | -.53 | -.21 | -.71 |
| POORVET | -1.10 | -.34 | .24 |

* Dummy variables: the listed category was coded 1, otherwise 0.

** Respondent's years of schooling minus father's years of schooling.

The discriminant function coefficients for the eight indicators show that this clear distinction between the new and veteran residents is based on differences in status and ethnocultural affiliations. The MILIT and CIVILNEW, particularly in comparison with POORVET, but also more than any other neighborhood group, are concentrated in prestigious occupations, are well educated, and also tend to be of European-American ancestry and to hold secular orientations.

While the first function provides a quite clear hierarchy of all groups in terms of status and ethnic group, the second and third functions are more specific, in the sense of distinguishing one particular neighborhood group from the rest. The second function mainly discriminates the CIVILVET from all other neighborhood groups. According to the discriminant coefficients, the veteran residents who moved into Newtown are revealed as a mobile group of a specific nature. They are relatively older, tend to be self-employed, and are educationally mobile compared with their fathers.

The third function mainly distinguishes between POORNEW and the other groups. This group, according to the discriminant function coefficients, tends to consist of employees in lower-prestige occupations, who are young and were born in Israel. These indicators, as we have seen earlier, indeed characterize the young families who moved into Poortown.

Generally, our analysis reveals two major facts about the neighborhood groups. First, it is evident that the "settle with us" project has created status and ethnic distinctions between the newcomers of Newtown and the rest of the residents, especially POORVET. Second, there is much variation in the sociodemographic profiles of specific neighborhood groups, both of veterans and of newcomers. In particular, our analysis emphasizes the social mobility of CIVILVET and the specific sociodemographic characteristics of the newcomers in Poortown. It is thus clear that there are sufficient sociological reasons to distinguish among the neighborhood groups in Mobiltown on the dual basis of geographical location and length of residence in the town.

## THE NEWCOMERS: PATTERNS OF MIGRATION TO MOBILTOWN

As we have seen, there are large sociodemographic variations not only between the newcomers and veteran groups of Mobiltown, but also among the newcomer groups themselves. The differences revealed among MILIT, CIVILNEW, MIDNEW, and POORNEW indicate that they may have settled down in Mobiltown for different reasons. Subsequently, each of these groups may regard its migration to the town in a different view, and this may affect its relations with the other new groups and veteran residents. It is therefore worthwhile to examine and compare the patterns of migration of the four new groups. We first depict the separate indicators of these patterns and then attempt to construct a combined migration profile of the four new groups.

### Present and Previous Residence

First, it should be pointed out that the four groups did not migrate to Mobiltown in exactly the same period of time. As shown in Table 3.6, the first newcomers were those of Midtown, followed much later by POORNEW and the Newtown residents. The newcomers of Newtown settled in Mobiltown some time after the mobile veterans moved into their new houses.

Consequently, the four new groups differ in the extent to which they use Mobiltown as a "bedroom suburb," or work there as well. Again combining the data for the respondents and their spouses, Table 3.6 presents, separately for the men and women of each group, a trichotomous distribution of work site: in Mobiltown (including those not working outside the home as a separate category), in the near vicinity (within a range of 20 kilometers from town), and farther. Although for all

**Table 3.6**
**Years of Residence and Work Sites by Neighborhood Group**

| | MILIT | CIVILNEW | CIVILVET | MIDNEW | MIDVET | POORNEW | POORVET |
|---|---|---|---|---|---|---|---|
| (a) Years of Residence at Present Address (N=568) | | | | | | | |
| Mean | 1.9 | 1.7 | 2.2* | 4.8 | 9.5* | 2.1 | 11.4* |
| S.D. | 2.2 | 1.1 | 1.2 | 9.4 | 7.1 | 1.5 | 7.9 |
| (b) Work Sites-Men | | | | | | | |
| In Mobiltown | 7.1 | 26.0 | 42.6 | 21.6 | 36.8 | 34.2 | 39.9 |
| Close to Mobiltown | 36.4 | 24.0 | 21.3 | 36.5 | 36.8 | 26.3 | 27.2 |
| Far away from Mobiltown | 54.5 | 46.0 | 31.9 | 35.1 | 21.1 | 34.2 | 21.5 |
| Not working outside home | 2.0 | 4.0 | 4.3 | 6.8 | 5.3 | 5.3 | 11.4 |
| Total** (N = 561) | 100.0% | 100.0% | 100.0% | 100.0% | 100.0% | 100.0% | 100.0% |
| (c) Work Sites - Women | | | | | | | |
| In Mobiltown | 18.8 | 22.4 | 31.9 | 31.5 | 38.9 | 16.7 | 42.9 |
| Near Mobiltown | 26.0 | 20.4 | 6.4 | 5.5 | 10.5 | 16.7 | 7.1 |
| Far away from Mobiltown | 15.6 | 18.4 | 8.5 | 13.7 | 1.1 | 8.3 | 2.6 |
| Not working outside home | 38.5 | 38.8 | 53.2 | 49.3 | 49.5 | 58.3 | 47.4 |
| Total** (N = 552) | 100.0% | 100.0% | 100.0% | 100.0% | 100.0% | 100.0% | 100.0% |

* For the veteran groups, years of residence at present address do not necessarily reflect years of residence in Mobiltown.

** In some cases the total is approximately 100% due to rounding errors.

neighborhood groups the proportion of women working outside Mobiltown is smaller than that of men, these differences among the groups are identical across gender. It is clear, first, that the proportion of residents working in town is higher among all veteran groups than among the newcomers. However, among the latter, those with a higher tendency of working in Mobiltown or its near vicinity are the newcomers of Midtown and Poortown. About half of the men in MILIT and CIVILNEW work far away from town.

**Table 3.7**
**Previous Residence of Newcomers by Neighborhood Group**

| | MILIT | CIVILNEW | MIDNEW | POORNEW |
|---|---|---|---|---|
| a. Area of Previous Residence | | | | |
| Near Mobiltown | 31.3 | 53.0 | 49.2 | 53.8 |
| Metropolitan Dan area | 35.4 | 42.9 | 26.0 | 20.5 |
| Far away from Mobiltown | 33.3 | 4.1 | 24.7 | 25.6 |
| Total* (N = 260) | 100.0% | 100.0% | 100.0% | 100.0% |
| b. Type of Previous Settlement | | | | |
| Large city | 20.2 | 23.3 | 17.9 | 13.5 |
| Middle-sized city | 50.0 | 67.4 | 46.4 | 64.9 |
| Small town | 11.7 | 2.3 | 17.9 | 8.2 |
| Other (development town, rural settlement) | 18.1 | 7.0 | 17.8 | 13.5 |
| Total* (N = 260) | 100.0% | 100.0% | 100.0% | 100.0% |

*In some cases the total is approximately 100% due to rounding errors.

Thus, among the newcomers the Newtown residents show the highest tendency of using Mobiltown as a "bedroom town." This may be related to the fact that they were the latest to arrive in town. At the same time, the life of a large portion of them is concentrated in Mobiltown and its vicinity. This is even more so among women, when we consider those women who do not work outside the home as "full-time" Mobiltowners.

The tendency of many newcomers to work far away from Mobiltown may also result from their personal preference to continue in the same jobs that they held prior to migration—in the businesses they owned or the managerial and military positions they held. This tendency is indicated by the comparison of geographical origins of the new groups. As shown in Table 3.7, MIDNEW and POORNEW mainly migrated from the middle-sized cities and towns in the near vicinity of Mobiltown. In contrast, CIVILNEW and MILIT more often came from the middle-sized and larger cities in the metropolitan Dan area (the urban area of Tel Aviv and its neighboring cities). Some of them might have migrated to Mobiltown with the intention of keeping their jobs or businesses, while using Mobiltown as a "bedroom town."

## Perceptions of Migration and Attraction

The different patterns of migration to Mobiltown are well reflected in the newcomers' own perceptions of the migration and its consequences. All the newcomers were asked to choose, from a prepared list, the major reason for their migration to Mobiltown and were then asked to evaluate their present housing and neighborhood in comparison to the ones prior to migration.

As shown in Table 3.8, the majority of CIVILNEW and a large part of MILIT contend that they moved to Mobiltown in order to improve their housing conditions. An additional quarter of MILIT attribute their migration to "economic opportunities," represented by the relatively inexpensive price of the houses in the military neighborhood subsequent to the cooperative contracting of builders. The reasons most often cited by the

**Table 3.8**
**Reasons for Migration to Mobiltown and Evaluation of Present Housing and Neighborhood**

| | MILIT | CIVILNEW | MIDNEW | POORNEW |
|---|---|---|---|---|
| (a) Major Reason of Migration to Mobiltown | | | | |
| Improving housing conditions | 41.9 | 68.8 | 14.5 | 16.7 |
| Economic opportunities | 23.7 | 6.3 | 56.5 | 33.3 |
| Family reasons | 1.1 | 6.3 | 13.0 | 38.9 |
| Being close to work | 14.0 | 6.3 | 13.0 | 5.6 |
| Quality of environment | 18.3 | 12.5 | 2.9 | 5.6 |
| Total* (N= 230) | 100.0% | 100.0% | 100.0% | 100.0% |
| (b) Evaluation of Present Housing | | | | |
| Better than previous | 88.7 | 91.9 | 56.9 | 46.9 |
| Same as previous | 8.2 | 8.1 | 26.2 | 18.8 |
| Worse than previous | 3.1 | 0.0 | 16.9 | 34.4 |
| Total* (N=226) | 100.0% | 100.0% | 100.0% | 100.0% |
| (c) Evaluation of Present Neighborhood | | | | |
| Better than previous | 81.1 | 76.5 | 46.9 | 18.8 |
| Same as previous | 15.8 | 17.6 | 35.9 | 28.1 |
| Worse than previous | 3.2 | 5.9 | 17.2 | 53.1 |
| Total* (N=225) | 100.0% | 100.0% | 100.0% | 100.0% |

* In some cases the total is approximately 100% due to rounding errors.

newcomers to Oldtown are quite different. The majority of MIDNEW and a third of POORNEW admit that their migration was due to financial opportunities. An even larger portion of POORNEW, who probably returned to Poortown to be closer to their parents, attribute their migration to family reasons.

It is clear, then, that the Newtowners were attracted to Mobiltown mainly by the opportunity to improve their housing conditions, while financial and family considerations stood behind the migration of the new Oldtowners. These different motivations are reflected in the evaluation of the different groups of their present housing and neighborhood, in comparison with the ones prior to migration. As Table 3.8 shows, the large majority of both MILIT and CIVILNEW believe that their present housing and neighborhood are better than their previous ones. The proportions of residents who share these beliefs among MIDNEW and POORNEW are much smaller. Actually, among POORNEW, many of whom returned to Poortown because their parents lived there, over a third state they moved into worse housing, and over half consider their present neighborhood worse than the one they used to live in.

Despite the above differences between the newcomers of Newtown and Oldtown, they still resemble each other in perceptions of life in Mobiltown, when compared with the veteran residents. Table 3.9 presents the responses of all seven neighborhood groups to a closed question, asking them to choose the major attraction of living in Mobiltown. The given choices distinguished between materialistic attractions (inexpensive and convenient life, adequate services) and social attractions (social contacts, an atmosphere of community, and "togetherness"). The respondents were also allowed to indicate their own unlisted attractions or to choose an additional given response stating that they are not attracted to living in Mobiltown.

The table shows that all four groups of newcomers chose, more often than the veteran groups, the option of "inexpensive and convenient life." The only exception to this materialistic view among the newcomers is MILIT. Since friendships among many of the military families who settled in Mobiltown existed

**Table 3.9**
**Attraction to Mobiltown and Perception of Its Influence on Personal Status by Neighborhood Group**

| | MILIT | CIVILNEW | CIVILVET | MIDNEW | MIDVET | POORNEW | POORVET |
|---|---|---|---|---|---|---|---|
| (a) Major Attraction of Living in Mobiltown | | | | | | | |
| Inexpensive and convenient | 22.7 | 30.0 | 12.8 | 32.0 | 18.4 | 28.2 | 18.8 |
| Adequate services | 7.2 | 16.0 | 4.3 | 8.0 | 21.4 | 2.6 | 1.2 |
| Social contacts | 18.6 | 10.0 | 17.0 | 6.7 | 15.5 | 10.3 | 15.6 |
| Community atmosphere | 20.6 | 18.0 | 23.4 | 6.7 | 12.6 | 2.6 | 8.1 |
| Other (e.g; family, work) | 2.4 | 10.0 | 31.9 | 9.3 | 14.6 | 17.9 | 18.5 |
| Unattracted to Mobiltown | 25.8 | 16.0 | 10.6 | 37.3 | 17.5 | 38.5 | 43.1 |
| Total* (N=571) | 100.0% | 100.0% | 100.0% | 100.0% | 100.0% | 100.0% | 100.0% |
| (b) Influence of Residence in Mobiltown on Personal Status | | | | | | | |
| Contributes to my social status | 9.1 | 8.0 | 25.5 | 6.7 | 21.4 | 10.3 | 17.8 |
| No influence | 89.9 | 88.0 | 72.3 | 76.0 | 73.8 | 82.1 | 72.6 |
| Lowers my social status | 1.0 | 4.0 | 2.1 | 17.3 | 4.9 | 7.7 | 9.6 |
| Total* (N=570) | 100.0% | 100.0% | 100.0% | 100.0% | 100.0% | 100.0% | 100.0% |

* In some cases the total is approximately 100% due to rounding errors.

prior to migration, they tend to emphasize the community atmosphere and the social contacts as major attractions of life in Mobiltown. In this respect, they resemble the mobile CIVILVET. All the other veteran groups show no particular preference for either the materialistic or the social types of attraction, though they chose "social contacts" more often than most newcomers. The only noteworthy pattern among the veterans is the tendency of POORVET to state that they are not attracted to Mobiltown. Such feelings were also expressed strongly by POORNEW and MIDNEW.

The tendency of most veterans to de-emphasize the community atmosphere of Mobiltown or its attractiveness altogether does not necessarily reflect a general low evaluation of Mobiltown as a place to live in. This was revealed when we asked the respondents whether being Mobiltown residents influences their personal status. As part b of Table 3.9 shows, most residents attributed no influence on their own social status to the town. However, the percentage of respondents who claimed that Mobiltown contributes to their social status was higher among all veteran groups (and in particular CIVILVET) than among the newcomers. The only group that shows a significant tendency toward the negative option (Mobiltown lowers personal status) is MIDNEW.

## Profiles of Migration

The discussion up to this point reveals different divisions or cutting points among the four newcomer groups in relation to the separate indicators of their migration patterns. Summing up these patterns requires the construction of migration profiles for the four groups. This was done by a discriminant analysis, in which the four groups were discriminated by all the factual and perceptional indicators of migration depicted above.

As Table 3.10 shows, three significant discriminant functions were produced. They are presented in order of their power of discrimination among the new neighborhood groups. The first, most powerful function distinguishes between the Newtown groups (especially MILIT, but also CIVILNEW) and the new groups in Oldtown (POORNEW, in particular). This is the distinction found most often when we dealt with the separate migration indicators. As the function coefficients indicate, the Newtowners are mainly characterized by a positive evaluation of their present neighborhood, while the Poortowners and, to some extent, the Midtowners hold a negative attitude toward their present neighborhoods. The latter groups migrated to Mobiltown because of family and financial constraints, while the Newtowners, as we have seen, came for other reasons.

The second and third functions concern specific new groups. The second distinguishes mainly between the MIDNEW and POORNEW groups. POORNEW, in contrast to the new Midtowners, came mainly from middle-sized cities in the vicinity of Mobiltown. The reason for their migration was their POORVET parents, while the new Midtowners were motivated to settle in Mobiltown primarily by economic opportunities. Therefore, the new Poortowners have a stronger tendency toward a negative evaluation of their neighborhood, though they tend to admit that Mobiltown contributes to their own social status in general.

The third function distinguishes CIVILNEW from the other three groups. As the function coefficients show, they tend to have come from areas relatively remote from Mobiltown (especially the metropolitan Dan area), but they tend to work in Mobiltown (this is more characteristic of the CIVILNEW women than of the men). Also, they tend to be attracted to living in Mobiltown, though they do not have many social contacts in town.

In general, the discriminant analysis further illuminates the heterogeneity of the four groups of Mobiltown newcomers with respect to their migration profiles: where they came from, the extent to which they use Mobiltown as a "bedroom town," their motivations for migration, and the reasons for which they find Mobiltown, in general and their neighborhood, in particular, attractive or unattractive to live in.

**Table 3.10**
**Discriminant Analysis: Profiles of Migration to Mobiltown (N=222)**

| Discriminating Variables and Standardized Discriminant Coefficients | Function 1 | Function 2 | Function 3 |
|---|---|---|---|
| Previous residential area: far away from Mobiltown* | -.05 | .10 | .58 |
| Previous residential area: near Mobiltown* | .17 | .45 | .17 |
| Type of previous settlement: large city* | -.02 | .42 | .10 |
| Type of previous settlement: middle-sized city* | -.01 | .50 | .04 |
| Work situs in Mobiltown* | .28 | .05 | -.63 |
| Work situs: close to Mobiltown* | .02 | .10 | -.01 |
| Work situs: not working outside home* | .29 | .01 | -.19 |
| Migration reason: improving housing conditions* | .03 | .22 | -.26 |
| Migration reason: economic opportunities* | .46 | -.49 | .06 |
| Migration reason: family reasons* | .55 | .20 | -.10 |
| Attraction to Mobiltown: inexpensive and convenient* | .03 | -.05 | .27 |
| Attraction to Mobiltown: social contacts* | -.16 | -.01 | .42 |
| Attraction to Mobiltown: community atmosphere* | -.17 | -.15 | .17 |
| Attraction to Mobiltown: unattracted* | -.11 | -.19 | .46 |
| Evaluation of present housing (1=worse than previous, 3=better) | -.19 | .29 | -.11 |

**Table 3.10 (continued)**

| Discriminating Variables and Standardized Discriminant Coefficients (continued) | Function 1 | Function 2 | Function 3 |
|---|---|---|---|
| Evaluation of present neighborhood (1=worse than previous, 3=better) | -.62 | -.39 | -.09 |
| Influence of Mobiltown on personal status (1=lowers social status, 3= contributes to status) | -.03 | .35 | .35 |
| Canonical correlation | .68 | .47 | .39 |
| Wilks' Lambda | .35 | .66 | .84 |
| P($x^2$ test) | <.001 | <.001 | .002 |
| MILIT | -.79 | .05 | .28 |
| CIVILNEW | -.53 | .53 | -.87 |
| MIDNEW | .61 | -.73 | -.16 |
| POORNEW | 1.76 | .76 | .28 |

* Dummy variables: the listed category was coded 1, otherwise 0.

## CONCLUSION: SOCIAL HIERARCHY, DISTINCT PROFILES

Our analysis of the neighborhood groups shows, first, that Mobiltown has indeed enhanced its status as a result of the "settle with us" project. In other words, the plan to attract higher status residents resulted in newcomers who, in comparison to the veterans, are generally more educated, are of a higher occupational prestige, and tend to be of Ashkenazi origin.

But the differences found were not only along the lines of newcomers versus veterans. Throughout our analysis it appears that all seven neighborhood groups differ from each other and exhibit distinct social profiles. First, it is evident that the seven groups form a clear social hierarchy, determined mainly by status characteristics. The newcomers of Newtown are at the top of this hierarchy, the veteran Poortowners are at the bottom, and the rest of the newcomers and veterans compose its middle echelons. In this sense, the "settle with us" project not only enhanced the status of Mobiltown, but has also created distinct status groups of the various combinations of neighborhood and length of residence.

Our claim that the neighborhood groups form distinct status groups is further substantiated by the analysis of the reasons for the newcomers' migration. We found significant variations in motivations for migration and in subsequent perceptions of life in Mobiltown among the four groups of newcomers. It appears that the planners of the demographic changes in Mobiltown have succeeded, under the ideological banner of social integration, in catering to different types of potential migrants. By offering different residential arrangements, they managed to bring into Mobiltown different groups of new residents—military families with their own friendship networks; successful civilians wishing to realize their dreams of luxurious private homes; other individuals who could inexpensively purchase an apartment in Midtown; and children of Poortowners, who could now return to the town and live close to their parents.

Both the socioeconomic hierarchy and the distinct migration profiles of the neighborhood groups indicate their formation as unique status groups. Status groups, as we have noted, are usually characterized by their exclusiveness and their potential of intergroup conflict. Yet, our neighborhood groups were brought together under the ideological umbrella of social integration. The question, then, is, Where does this unique combination of integrative ideology and status group separation lead Mobiltown? What kinds of lifestyles and friendship networks do the various neighborhood groups develop as a result? How do they perceive each other and relate to their integration within the same community? In our exploration of these issues in the following chapters, we attempt to cope with our main theoretical dilemma: does status enhancement of a community, carried out under an integrative ideology, result in social integration or, rather, in social separation and conflict?

# 4

# Lifestyle and Friendship Networks

Our analysis up to this point has indicated that the various neighborhood groups have a sufficient basis for forming distinct status groups: they have unique socioeconomic characteristics and different reasons for being in Mobiltown. The question is whether such status groups are formed in reality.

This chapter addresses the question of status group formation by focusing on the lifestyles and friendship patterns developed within the neighborhood groups. Lifestyle is a central element in the formation of status groups. In explaining Max Weber's theory of social stratification, Randall Collins (1986:134) writes: "Status groups (at least in the upper ranks)... build a lifestyle and a community organization out of their wealth. They also use it as their claim to social eminence." Hence, close friendship networks among members of a neighborhood group indicate their cohesion as a status group.

Lifestyles are measured in our analysis by consumption patterns in various life areas. The more the residents of specific neighborhood groups share common consumption patterns that differ from those of other groups, the more they form a lifestyle of a status group. Also, the more they limit their friendships to group members, the more cohesive their status group. Obviously, unique lifestyles and within-group friendship networks increase the probability of social separation among the neighborhood groups. Social integration of the various groups means similarities in their lifestyles and the dispersion of friendship networks across neighborhood groups.

The investigation of lifestyles addresses an additional aspect, related to the status enhancement of Mobiltown. Patterns of consumption indicate the utilization of community resources. In a development town such as Mobiltown, various consumption behaviors in the areas of culture and commerce may have been introduced by the newcomers. However, cultural and commercial consumption may be carried out either in Mobiltown or outside it, in larger urban centers. The more the patterns of consumption concentrate in Mobiltown, the more effective its status enhancement will be. Thus, we must examine whether the status enhancement process has developed Mobiltown as a commercial and cultural center for its residents or has rather turned it into a "bedroom town," the residents of which prefer to concentrate their activities outside the community. If this is the outcome, then the demographic change of Mobiltown represents merely an increase of the number of residents, but not a significant change in the structure of the community.

## PATTERNS OF CONSUMPTION

The first part of the analysis deals with cultural consumption—participation in cultural activities and services. The mere consumption of culture, as well as its characteristics, is a central source of differentiation between status groups (Bourdieu and Passeron, 1977; DiMaggio, 1982). The main questions in this context are: Do the neighborhood groups differ in their patterns of cultural consumption? Do they consume different cultural services?

Consumption of commercial services is another basic indicator of lifestyle, and here, too, we are interested in patterns of differentiation. The crucial issue is whether Mobiltown crystallizes as a cultural and service center for its inhabitants or the inhabitants are still dependent for these services on outside centers. This issue is especially relevant to the newcomers.

## Who Consumes What?

The analysis of patterns of consumption is presented in the "A" category of Table 4.1. The differentiation among the neighborhood groups in terms of patterns of consumption is not uniform. In several domains there is no significant difference between the neighborhood groups. This pertains mostly, but not solely, to everyday consumption (groceries, clothing, shoes, and the like). In addition to everyday consumption, we find only negligible differences in use of swimming pool, videotape library, bank services, and purchasing of books, toys, and records. It might seem surprising that groups that are clearly differentiated in terms of socioeconomic characteristics exhibit similar patterns of consumption in many domains. This may indicate the relatively high living standards in Mobiltown. Services such as bank, swimming pool, and bookshops are not perceived as a privilege of the higher-status groups.

The most prominent difference between Newtown and Oldtown is revealed in cultural consumption. MILIT and CIVILNEW exhibit a notable tendency to participate in cultural activities, thus establishing their identity as status groups with distinct cultural styles. These same groups, together with CIVILVET, are the main users of the library. In other cultural activities, both those organized for adults and those for children, the differences between the groups are residual and nonsystematic.

The higher economic status of the Newtowners is expressed in two areas—summer camps and car repair services. The Newtowners, especially MILIT, are those who tend to send their children to summer camps. Strikingly high proportions (over 90 percent) of MILIT and CIVILNEW use car repair services, which probably indicates the ownership of a car, a valid indicator of economic status in Israel.

It is important to note that POORVET, the lowest socioeconomic status group, does not exhibit unique patterns of consumption. In most areas it does not differ significantly from other veteran residents. Another interesting finding is that

**Table 4.1**
**Patterns of Consumption of the Neighborhood Groups**

| | | MILIT | CIVILNEW | CIVILVET | MIDNEW | MIDVET | POORNEW | POORVET |
|---|---|---|---|---|---|---|---|---|
| **Cultural Activities** (N=572) | A | 78.8 | 77.6 | 44.7 | 36.0 | 33.0 | 53.8 | 33.8 |
| | B | 31.2 | 73.6 | 66.7 | 33.3 | 38.2 | 28.6 | 40.7 |
| **Adult Clubs** (N=556) | A | 37.1 | 21.7 | 25.4 | 23.5 | 10.3 | 15.8 | 38.8 |
| | B | 80.6 | 89.5 | 87.5 | 100.0 | 87.5 | 100.0 | 91.7 |
| **Youth Clubs** (N=484) | A | 76.6 | 69.4 | 81.8 | 35.6 | 61.8 | 21.6 | 51.8 |
| | B | 97.2 | 100.0 | 100.0 | 100.0 | 94.5 | 100.0 | 98.3 |
| **Bank Services** (N=573) | A | 100.0 | 98.0 | 97.9 | 100.0 | 99.0 | 97.4 | 98.8 |
| | B | 50.5 | 9.2 | 95.7 | 77.3 | 93.1 | 71.0 | 96.8 |
| **Car Repair Services** (N=562) | A | 94.8 | 94.0 | 75.6 | 48.6 | 59.4 | 51.3 | 44.9 |
| | B | 23.9 | 19.1 | 73.5 | 33.3 | 51.7 | 45.0 | 58.6 |
| **Hair-dresser** (N=568) | A | 99.0 | 90.0 | 93.6 | 86.5 | 95.1 | 92.3 | 86.6 |
| | B | 60.2 | 66.7 | 95.5 | 75.0 | 84.5 | 77.8 | 86.8 |
| **Summer Camps** (N=562) | A | 83.8 | 73.5 | 76.6 | 41.9 | 65.7 | 51.3 | 47.7 |
| | B | 49.4 | 69.4 | 94.4 | 67.7 | 78.5 | 75.0 | 81.1 |
| **Library** (N=569) | A | 94.0 | 76.0 | 91.5 | 62.2 | 69.3 | 53.8 | 57.0 |
| | B | 70.2 | 71.1 | 95.3 | 65.2 | 87.1 | 66.7 | 83.3 |
| **Swimming Pool** (N=568) | A | 92.9 | 87.8 | 91.3 | 82.4 | 87.3 | 82.1 | 75.0 |
| | B | 24.2 | 60.5 | 86.0 | 62.3 | 83.1 | 78.1 | 79.2 |

**Table 4.1** (cont.)

| | | MILIT | CIVILNEW | CIVILVET | MIDNEW | MIDVET | POORNEW | POORVET |
|---|---|---|---|---|---|---|---|---|
| **Videotape Library** (N=564) | A | 27.6 | 30.0 | 19.1 | 16.2 | 35.0 | 28.9 | 24.8 |
| | B | 22.2 | 20.0 | 77.8 | 58.3 | 65.7 | 90.9 | 71.8 |
| **Purchase of Children's Books & Toys** (N=565) | A | 93.9 | 95.9 | 97.9 | 78.8 | 84.8 | 94.7 | 69.0 |
| | B | 40.9 | 46.8 | 65.9 | 55.9 | 66.7 | 55.6 | 73.4 |
| **Purchase of Books & Records** (N=568) | A | 91.8 | 89.4 | 84.0 | 81.2 | 87.2 | 69.8 | 93.9 |
| | B | 13.3 | 32.6 | 54.8 | 27.0 | 47.6 | 47.1 | 55.0 |
| **Groceries*** (N=573) | B | 93.0 | 92.0 | 100.0 | 96.0 | 98.1 | 92.3 | 98.1 |
| **Purchase of Household Products*** (N=570) | B | 50.0 | 75.5 | 93.6 | 76.0 | 95.1 | 84.6 | 95.6 |
| **Purchase of Clothes & Shoes*** (N=566) | B | 18.6 | 27.7 | 55.3 | 45.3 | 55.9 | 53.8 | 67.3 |
| **Purchase of Expensive Items*** (N=562) | B | 6.1 | 4.0 | 19.6 | 11.0 | 33.7 | 33.3 | 47.4 |

Note: For each activity or item, A is the percent of neighborhood group's respondents who participate or consume the item in general; B is the percent of respondents who participate or consume the item in Mobiltown, out of total participants or consumers.
* A is omitted since consumption is general.

despite the move to Newtown, CIVILVET remains distinct as a neighborhood in terms of lifestyle.

## Who Consumes Where?

As we have seen, the answer to "Who consumes what?" is that everyone consumes almost everything. The answer to "Who consumes where?" seems to be different. Apparently, the neighborhood groups are differentiated to a much greater extent in terms of place of consumption. These patterns are presented in category "B" of Table 4.1.

The most prominent conclusion of this part of the table is the apparent tendency of new inhabitants in Newtown, especially MILIT, to use services out of Mobiltown. CIVILVET act similarly to veteran Oldtowners, who tend to prefer Mobiltown's services. MIDNEW appears as an intermediate group. They use Mobiltown's services more than the new Newtowners, but less than veteran inhabitants. The additional group of new residents, POORNEW, is closer in this respect to the veterans. As previously noted, many POORNEW are offspring of veteran inhabitants who have returned to Mobiltown. This may explain their similarity to veterans rather than to other newcomers in terms of place of consumption.

## Profiles of Consumers

Having established that the neighborhood groups vary in terms of place of consumption, we now want to clarify and systematize that differentiation. To do so, we performed a discriminant analysis that creates profiles of the neighborhood groups in terms of place of consumption.

**Table 4.2**
**Discriminant Analysis: Consumption in Mobiltown or Outside It (N=443)**

| Discriminating Variables and Standardized Discriminant Coefficients | Function 1 | Function 2 |
|---|---|---|
| Groceries | -.07 | .13 |
| Household products | .49 | -.50 |
| Clothes | .10 | .28 |
| Big shopping | .06 | .75 |
| Toys | -.06 | .37 |
| Books | .10 | -.59 |
| Bank services | .40 | .32 |
| Hairdresser | .01 | .24 |
| Swimming pool | .49 | -.34 |
| Canonical Correlation | .65 | .32 |
| Wilks' Lambda | .48 | .08 |
| p ($x^2$ test) | <.05 | <.05 |
| **Group Centroids** | | |
| MILIT | 1.50 | -.15 |
| CIVILNEW | .15 | .74 |
| CIVILVET | -.57 | .22 |
| MIDNEW | .71 | .42 |
| MIDVET | -.40 | .27 |
| POORNEW | .07 | .00 |
| POORVET | -.60 | .05 |

* All variables are dummy variables: consumption in Mobiltown was coded "0," outside it, "1."

The discriminant analysis (Table 4.2) again demonstrates the high degree of differentiation between the neighborhood groups. Two statistically significant functions are obtained. The first is based on the utilization of the everyday services offered by Mobiltown (house utilities, bank, swimming pool). The main differentiation provided by this function is between MILIT and all other groups. Inhabitants of the military quarter exhibit an apparent tendency to prefer services out of Mobiltown. Since we are dealing here with army officers, it is quite plausible that they use the special department stores where members of the Israeli defense forces are granted a discount. Three groups exhibit a higher tendency to prefer those services inside Mobiltown: CIVILVET, MIDVET, and, to a certain extent, POORNEW.

The second function differentiates CIVILNEW from the other groups. This function is based on a combination of nonfrequent services—expensive purchases, made in Mobiltown—and frequent purchases, such as household products, which are made outside.

The analysis indicates different patterns of consumption. However, these are not accounted for merely by length of residence. The tendency to prefer Mobiltown's commercial services is somewhat higher among long-term residents. However, their inner differentiation, and that revealed among the newcomers, indicate that neighborhood groups of similar seniority develop different patterns of consumption.

## Satisfaction with Services

The variation among the neighborhood groups in terms of patterns of consumption, as well as their differentiation in terms of socioeconomic characteristics, raises the issue of their satisfaction with the town services. This is presented in Table 4.3. The table indicates that it is impossible to depict one general pattern of satisfaction. Apparently, Mobiltowners react differently to different services.

Mobiltowners appear quite satisfied with the educational services. About 80 percent of the total sample are at least satisfied with these services. The differentiation among the neighborhood groups is negligible. Apparently, the education system of Mobiltown is perceived as a success by both veterans and newcomers. Mobiltowners also respond most positively to their religious services. This is true especially for Oldtowners. The exceptional group in this area is MILIT, which exhibits the

**Table 4.3**
**Satisfaction With Services by Neighborhood Group**

Percent Satisfied and Very Satisfied

| | Education | Culture | Welfare | Sanitation | Health | Religious | General Satisfaction |
|---|---|---|---|---|---|---|---|
| **Newtown** | | | | | | | |
| MILIT | 82.3 | 25.0 | 84.3 | 58.6 | 53.9 | 51.7 | 86.9 |
| CIVILNEW | 81.8 | 7.1 | 85.7 | 50.0 | 57.1 | 77.8 | 89.8 |
| CIVILVET | 84.8 | 53.7 | 67.6 | 52.2 | 61.7 | 85.4 | 91.5 |
| **Oldtown** | | | | | | | |
| MIDNEW | 87.7 | 8.9 | 71.8 | 73.0 | 70.5 | 93.0 | 69.4 |
| MIDVET | 85.8 | 47.8 | 70.6 | 67.7 | 70.0 | 93.4 | 82.2 |
| POORNEW | 71.6 | 37.1 | 61.0 | 42.5 | 78.5 | 92.3 | 63.1 |
| POORVET | 88.5 | 23.3 | 59.3 | 35.9 | 74.3 | 96.0 | 59.0 |
| TOTAL | 80.9 | 39.7 | 67.8 | 54.7 | 68.8 | 88.9 | 75.8 |
| N | 489 | 469 | 373 | 570 | 538 | 378 | 570 |

lowest degree of satisfaction (about 50 percent satisfied compared with more than 90 percent among Oldtowners). This might stem from MILIT's resentment of the ethnic character of the synagogues in Mobiltown. All synagogues belong to narrowly defined ethnic groups (Moroccans, Yemenites, and so forth). As nontraditional Jews, typical of the Ashkenazi middle class, MILIT are interested in nonethnic religious services. Indeed, shortly after this survey, MILIT founded their own nonethnic synagogue.

Average levels of satisfaction are attached to health services, welfare services, and sanitation. The reaction to health services distinguishes between Oldtowners and Newtowners, with the former expressing higher levels of satisfaction. In terms of sanitation, the dissatisfaction of the inhabitants of Poortown is apparent. As a distressed neighborhood, the local services provided to them are below average. Mobiltowners are quite dissatisfied with the cultural services in their town. This is particularly prominent among MILIT, the main cultural consumers, and among POORVET.

The general attitude toward Mobiltown is depicted by the item that pertains to general satisfaction. Here a clear distinction emerges between Newtowners and Oldtowners. Newtowners, with only minor inner differentiation, are quite satisfied with life in Mobiltown. Oldtowners, and particularly the Poortowners, are less content.

In most areas analyzed in this section, the main source of differentiation is the neighborhoods. Length of residence has no significant effect. This pattern is not surprising; since most services are directly attached to the neighborhoods, the reaction of the respondents expresses their attitude toward services in the quarters they live in.

## Effect of Neighborhood Group on Patterns of Consumption

As noted, the neighborhood groups are highly differentiated in terms of socioeconomic characteristics. Hence, the divergent

**Figure 4.1**
**Factors Affecting General Patterns of Consumption: The Linear Structural Relations Model**

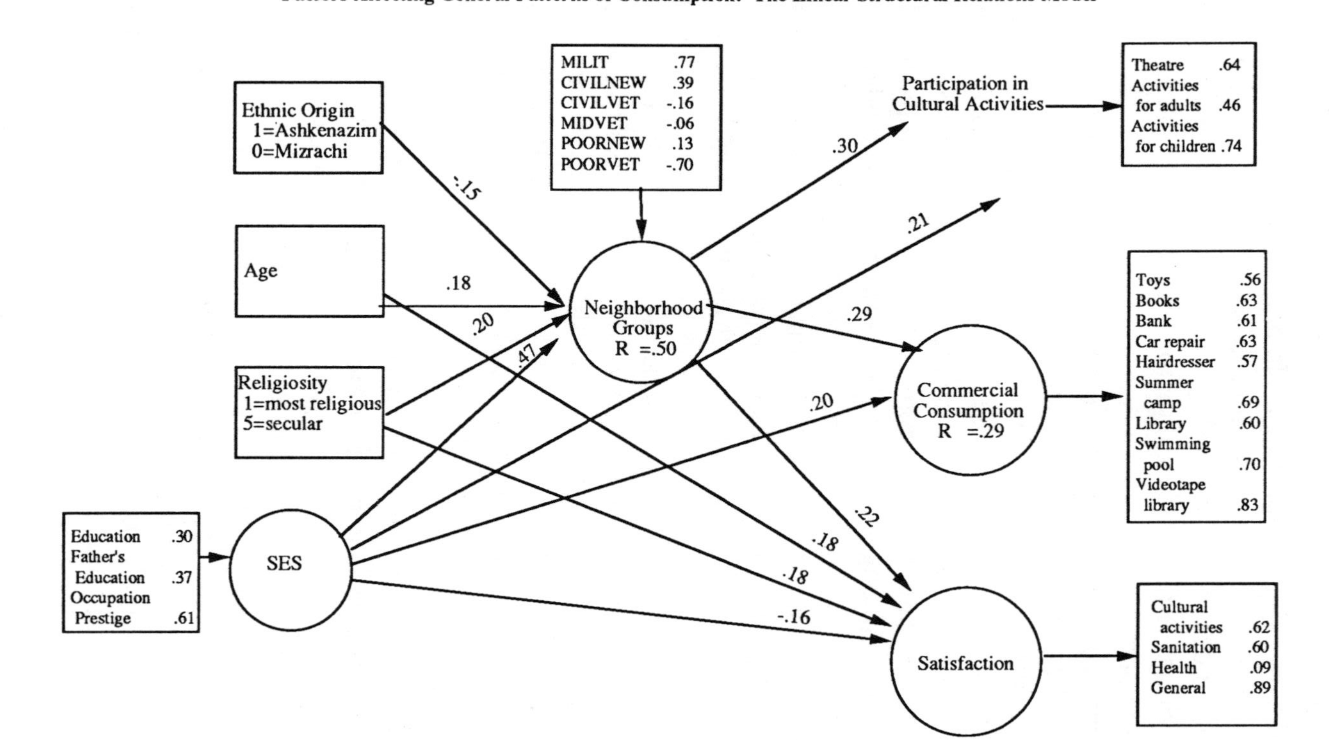


Note: Correlations among the exogenous variables and among the dependent variables and path coefficients lower than .15 are omitted from the figure. Gender, which has no other path coefficients, is not presented, although included in the analysis.

patterns of consumption of the various groups might be attached to their individual characteristics rather than to their neighborhood group affiliation. In order to test this proposition, we apply the linear structural relations model, which incorporates neighborhood group membership along with individual traits as explanatory factors of patterns of consumption.

The dependent variables in the first model (Figure 4.1) are cultural consumption, consumption of commercial services, and satisfaction with services. The items that represent each of these dependent variables are those that were found to differentiate among neighborhood groups in the preliminary analyses. Due to the large number of original items, we excluded the nondifferentiating ones in order to simplify the model. The model is a path analytic one, in which neighborhood groups mediate between the background characteristics, which constitute the independent variables, and the dependent factors.

The neighborhood group is an inwardly directed construct. Hence, the weights of the various items that compose it are interpreted as regression coefficients (beta). These beta values indicate that the construct is affected by MILIT (positively) and by POORVET (negatively). CIVILNEW has a moderate positive effect on the construct. The remaining groups (MIDNEW serves as a comparison group in the construct and hence is omitted from the presentation of the construct) have no meaningful effect.

The model again demonstrates the sharp differentiation between the various groups in terms of individual-level traits. These are responsible for 50 percent of the construct's variance. The central trait is socioeconomic status (b =.47), indicating the higher status of the new residents in Newtown. The effects of the additional explanatory variables are secondary to socioeconomic status.

Obviously, our main interest is in the net effect of neighborhood groups on patterns of consumption. Each of the dependent variables is an outwardly directed construct. The

**Figure 4.2**
**Factors Affecting Consumption in Mobiltown: The Linear Structural Relations Model**

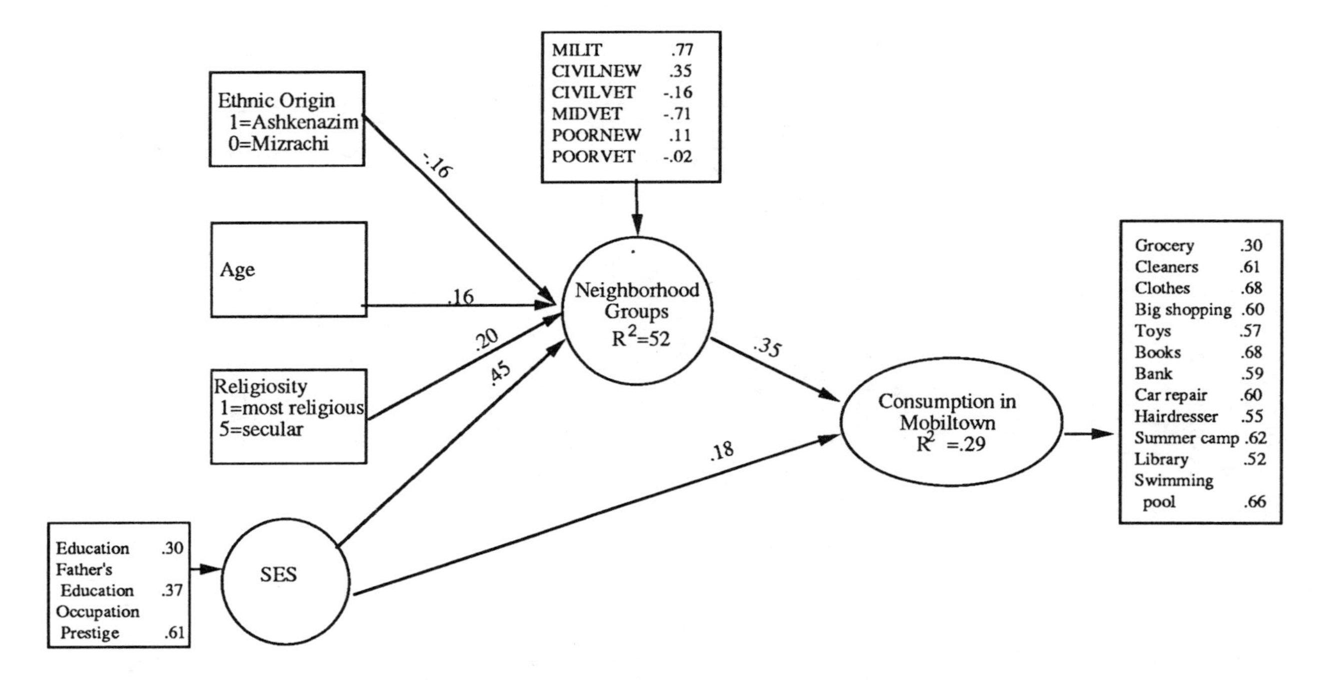


Note: Correlations among the exogenous variables and among the dependent variables and path coefficients lower than .15 are omitted from the figure. Gender, which has no other path coefficients, is not presented, although included in the analysis.

items that compose each construct appear in the respective rectangle.

The neighborhood group appears as the central variable in the shaping of consumption of both cultural and commercial services, but socioeconomic status retains an independent significant effect on each. New inhabitants in Newtown are the major consumers of both cultural and commercial services. However, higher status residents of Mobiltown, regardless of both neighborhood and length of residence, are also frequent consumers. No additional variable has any significant effect on the patterns of consumption.

The explanatory power of the model in terms of satisfaction with services is relatively low ($R^2$ =.12, whereas it reaches the value of .29 when consumption of commercial services is dependent and .22 in explaining consumption of cultural services). Here the effect of neighborhood groups only slightly exceeds the effects of the individual level variables. It appears that new inhabitants in Newtown express higher levels of satisfaction. A similar tendency is revealed among the older residents, the more religious, and those with the higher SES. However, the total effect of all variables is quite weak and should be interpreted as marginal.

The second model (Figure 4.2) concentrates only on those who report the use of commercial services, and it differentiates the inhabitants in terms of place of consumption. The explanatory power of the model is quite high ($R^2$ =.33).

The centrality of neighborhood groups in this domain is straightforward. The beta value pertaining to the construct is high (b =.35), indicating the tendency of new residents in Newtown to use commercial services outside Mobiltown.

An additional variable that appears to affect the dependent variable is socioeconomic status. Higher status inhabitants exhibit less tendency to use the commercial services inside Mobiltown. However, the effect is small and is certainly secondary to that of neighborhood groups.

## FRIENDSHIP NETWORKS

The formation of friendships among inhabitants is a basic feature in community life. Concerning the issue of status groups, social relations inside the neighborhood groups may serve as a powerful indicator of their cohesiveness. Close contacts between members of the neighborhood group might facilitate the formation of a unique lifestyle. Moreover, these contacts are providers of social power, since they facilitate inner organization aimed at the achievement of goals. This improves the group's bargaining power. Consequently, we can expect a group characterized by many friendship networks to better utilize the resources of the community.

The formation of friendship networks has an additional meaning for the analysis of life in Mobiltown. Social contacts between members of the community would prevent Mobiltown from becoming merely a "bedroom town" for its inhabitants. Most significant for our analysis is the nature of the friendship networks. As we already know, Newtown is quite separated from Oldtown. Since the physical separation is accompanied by a notable degree of socioeconomic differentiation, we can expect most friendship networks to be based on the neighborhoods. This may certainly contribute to social distance and segregation, thereby negating the general aim of social integration.

As noted, the survey was conducted only a few years after the initial settlement of Newtown. Hence, it might be argued that established friendship networks can be expected mainly among the Oldtowners. Yet, we must keep in mind that many residents of the military quarter arrived in Mobiltown on a group basis. Thus the issue of friendship networks is relevant to both Newtowners and Oldtowners.

### Who Socializes With Whom?

The formation of friendship networks is analyzed through three aspects. Do the respondents have friends in Mobiltown? What is the neighborhood membership of those friends? Are they newcomers or long-term residents? The patterns of the neighborhood groups pertaining to these aspects are presented in Table 4.4.

**Table 4.4**
**Distribution of Friendship Networks by Neighborhood Group (Percents)**

| | Have Friends in Mobiltown | Have Friends in Same Neighborhood | Most Friends New in Mobiltown |
|---|---|---|---|
| **Newtown** | | | |
| MILIT | 90.0 | 90.2 | 92.3 |
| CIVILNEW | 94.0 | 83.3 | 69.8 |
| CIVILVET | 97.9 | 28.6 | 11.7 |
| | | | |
| **Oldtown** | | | |
| MIDNEW | 82.4 | 55.9 | 50.0 |
| MIDVET | 87.3 | 56. | 4.7 |
| POORNEW | 79.5 | 66.7 | 32.8 |
| POORVET | 83.7 | 52.8 | 7.6 |
| | | | |
| Total (N=485) | 87.1 | 63.4 | 35.2 |

Note: Percentages in each cell are calculated out of total respondents in each neighborhood group.

The table indicates the existence of definite patterns. It appears that only a small minority report no friendships in Mobiltown. Inhabitants of the poor neighborhoods, both veterans and newcomers, and MIDNEW have less social relations in Mobiltown. The highest level of social involvement is expressed by the Newtowners. Apparently, the shorter period of residence in Mobiltown does not reduce the extent of friendship networks among the newcomers. This is not surprising as far as MILIT is concerned. As noted, many of them joined Mobiltown as friendship groups. What is astonishing is the finding of extensive social contacts of CIVILNEW. These newcomers settled in Mobiltown on an individual basis, so their social contacts there probably followed their arrival in the town. CIVILNEW's social contacts provide the most valid indication of the intensity of social life in Newtown.

The distribution of the friendship networks according to neighborhood location yields greater variation. Two groups report a high level of in-neighborhood contacts—these are the new inhabitants in Newtown. On the other hand, CIVILVET maintains most of the friendship networks with Oldtowners. The four additional groups have mixed networks—more than half of their friends come from their own neighborhood, but they still report many cross-neighborhood relationships.

The distinction of the friends according to length of residence reveals the tendency to form homogeneous networks. The only inhabitants whose networks are more heterogeneous are POORNEW and MIDNEW. Evidently, newcomers in veteran neighborhoods have better chances of meeting both newcomers and long-term residents.

This part of the analysis indicates that new inhabitants in Newtown form the most "local" friendship networks. The most "open" to various friendships are the other newcomers who have friends outside their own neighborhood and who associate with long-term residents.

## The Effect of Neighborhood Groups

The new residents in Newtown tend to be the most resistant to heterogeneous relationships in terms of both neighborhood affiliation and length of residence. In order to assess the net effect of neighborhood group affiliation on these relationships, we need to control for the effect of individual traits, such as socioeconomic status, ethnicity, and religiosity. Of particular interest is the individual status effect, because of the prominent socioeconomic gaps among residents in the different neighborhoods. This control is obtained by applying the linear

**Figure 4.3**
**Factors Affecting Formation of Friendship Networks: The Linear Structural Relations Model**

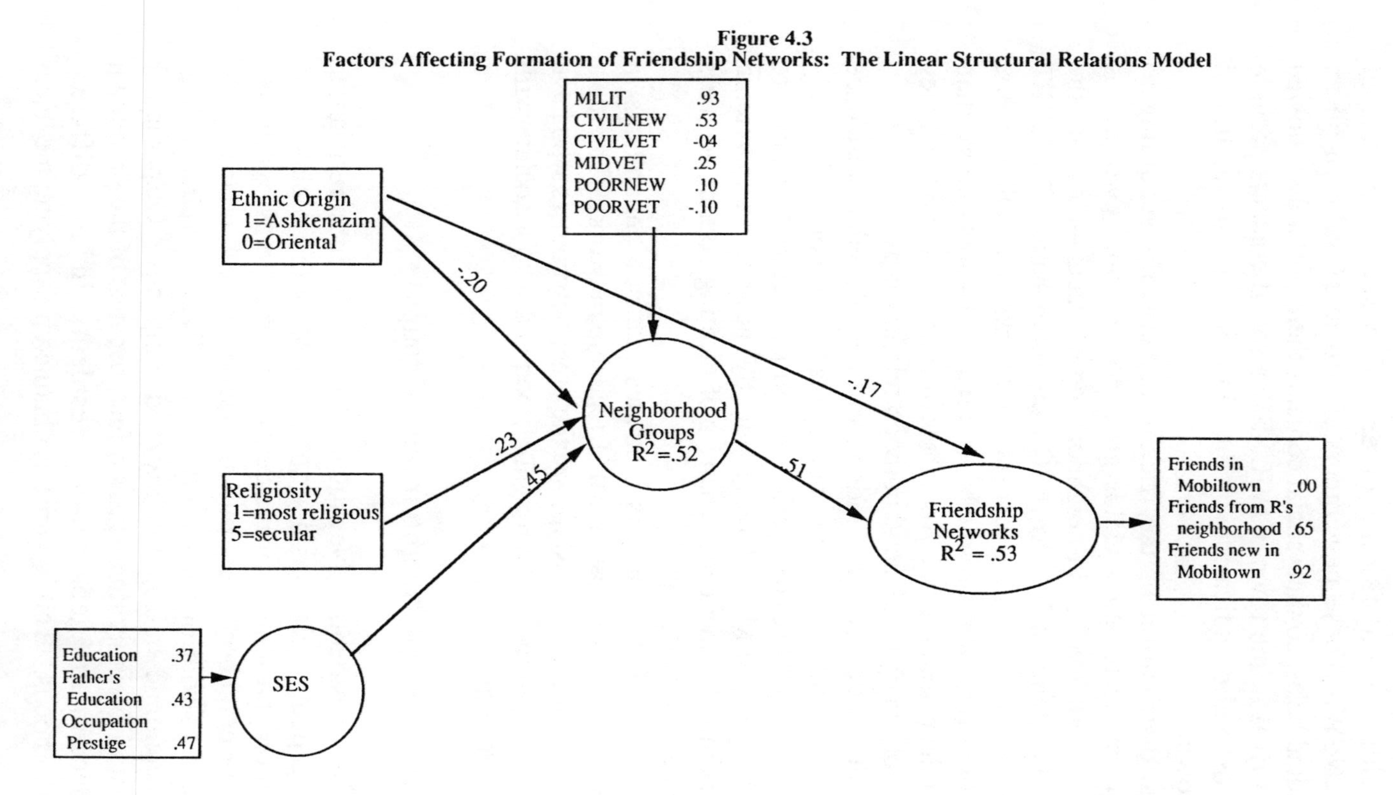


NOTE: Correlations among the exogeneous variables and among the dependent variables, and path coefficients lower than .15, are omitted from the figure. Age and gender which have no other path coefficients are not presented, although included in the analysis.

structural relations model. The findings are presented in Figure 4.3.

The three friendship aspects that were analyzed separately in the previous section compose the "friendship networks" construct. The construct is heavily loaded only by length of residence and neighborhood location. The explanatory power of the model is quite impressive ($R^2$ =.53). The central variable in the formation of patterns of friendship networks is neighborhood groups. New inhabitants in Newtown, especially MILIT, are characterized by friends who belong to their category in terms of neighborhood group membership. The rest of the groups, especially the veterans, resemble each other in friendship patterns that are less focused on the neighborhood. As noted earlier, CIVILVET resembles the Oldtowners, rather than the Newtowners, in this respect.

The only individual-level variable that has some significant effect on "friendship networks" is ethnic origin. Inhabitants of Ashkenazi origin have more friends who are new in Mobiltown and who live in the same neighborhood. Mizrachim exhibit some tendency toward veteran friends. Beyond this quite marginal effect, individual-level characteristics, including socioeconomic status, religiosity, age, and gender, have no significant independent influence on friendship networks. However, socioeconomic status and religiosity influence the friendship networks indirectly through their effect on the neighborhood group construct.

## CONCLUSIONS

Two questions guided the empirical analysis in this chapter. Do the various neighborhood groups exhibit unique lifestyles and segregative friendship networks, indicating the formation of distinct status groups? Do the consumption patterns of the various groups reflect the development of Mobiltown as a cultural and commercial center, or do they indicate that the attempt to enhance the status of the community ends up in the creation of a "bedroom community"?

Both the consumption patterns and the friendship networks indicate that the neighborhood groups tend to form status groups. Though we did not find significant differences among the groups in everyday consumption, we discovered large differences in cultural participation and, to some extent, in specific areas of commercial consumption. The differences were mainly pronounced in the comparison of MILIT and CIVILNEW with the other groups. While these differences may be attributed to variations in socioeconomic status, our multivariate analysis shows that neighborhood group affiliation still influences these consumption differences after socioeconomic status is taken into account. This means that the neighborhood groups, indeed, serve as status frameworks for their inhabitants, especially with respect to cultural activity.

The findings were similar and even stronger with regard to friendship networks. The most striking finding concerns the social "closure" of the new residents in Newtown. This is especially true of MILIT, but also of CIVILNEW. Although these groups of newcomers have many social relations inside the community, they are limited to other members of their own neighborhoods. Other newcomers, who did not join Mobiltown in the framework of the "settle with us" project, seem to be much more open to relations with long-term residents. Actually, MILIT and CIVILNEW are the only groups with strictly in-neighborhood relations. The veteran residents, both in Newtown and in Oldtown, exhibit stronger tendencies of cross-neighborhood friendships.

The unique consumption patterns and social closure of MILIT and CIVILNEW may certainly increase their power in the community as prestigious status groups. This is liable to lower the chances of social integration in Mobiltown, especially if the new Newtowners are able to get organized for the attainment of their specific goals.

The distinction between the neighborhood groups is also prominent in terms of place of consumption. New residents in

Newtown tend not to utilize the services offered by Mobiltown. This low level of resource utilization probably stems from their dissatisfaction with the cultural and commercial services in Mobiltown. In terms of potential long-term effects, this may lead in one of two directions. One possibility is that the newcomers will continue to use the commercial and cultural centers of larger cities, thus turning Mobiltown into their "bedroom town." However, their crystallization as status groups may lead the Newtowners to initiate the establishment of new and more appropriate services. The foundation of the new nonethnic synagogue, the construction of the new luxurious commercial center, and the opening of high-standard restaurants are good examples of such a process. If this is the direction of future developments, we shall be able to consider the status enhancement process as beneficial for neighborhood groups of the entire community, even though it led to the crystallization of prestigious and segregative status groups.

# 5

# How Groups View Each Other

Our analysis has demonstrated that the neighborhood groups bear some characteristics of status groups from an objective point of view: their socioeconomic distinctions, migration profiles, lifestyles, and friendship patterns all indicate this. The question we raise in this chapter is, How are these characteristics reflected in the subjective attitudes of the neighborhood groups toward themselves and toward each other?

The concept of status groups emphasizes the primary importance of resources and power in intergroup relations. Accordingly, the encounter between people of various groups is expected to raise group prejudice and negative mutual perceptions of the various groups. This may negate the conception of the "settle with us" project as a scheme of social integration.

On the other hand, the unique characteristics of the status enhancement process may lead us to different predictions regarding the mutual attitudes of the neighborhood groups. Status enhancement programs, such as the "settle with us" project of Mobiltown, strengthen the status of the weaker groups in the integrated situation: while the stronger newcomers were granted material facilities in accordance with their wealth and position, these facilities were controlled by a political elite that represents the weaker veteran population. This possible reversal of power may compensate for the status differences among the groups, thereby producing a more egalitarian setting in Mobiltown.

At the theoretical level, this status enhancement process may lead to expectations derived from sociopsychological theories of intergroup relations. In particular, the contact hypothesis (Brewer and Kramer, 1985; Brewer and Miller, 1984; Hewstone and Brown, 1986) assumes that more egalitarian circumstances of the encounter between people of different groups weaken their intergroup prejudices and increase the chances of developing egalitarian intergroup relations.

In order to examine which of the two directions applies in Mobiltown, we study relevant collective perceptions and images. Specifically, we examine whether Mobiltowners view themselves as divided into different categories or groups in a socially significant manner. If they do, we explore the labels they use to describe their divisions—ethnic, social, ecological, or others. Do they interpret these divisions in terms of unequal power and influence? Do they share stereotyped images of each other? How do they perceive the present relations in the community?

## PERCEPTIONS OF SOCIAL BOUNDARIES

We used open-ended questions regarding both the issue of the existence of social divisions and the criteria of differentiation in Mobiltown. This was done to allow expression of the widest range of possibilities and to find out whether our neighborhood group divisions are socially significant according to the residents' own perceptions.

As shown in part a of Table 5.1, Mobiltowners do see themselves as divided into different groups. This view is widely accepted by Mobiltowners but is particularly emphasized by MILIT.

Regarding the criteria of division, however, the answers are more diverse. As shown in part b of the table, some refer to class differences, that is, rich versus poor, successful versus unsuccessful, salaried workers versus employers or self-employed persons. Others mention ethnic cleavages—Ashkenazi versus Oriental Jews, or specific ethnic groups. Still

**Table 5.1**
**Perceptions of Groups in Mobiltown**

| | MILIT | CIVILNEW | CIVILVET | MIDNEW | MIDVET | POORNEW | POORVET |
|---|---|---|---|---|---|---|---|
| (a) Percentage agreeing: Different groups exist in Mobiltown (N=549) | 72.6 | 63.8 | 59.6 | 58.5 | 58.8 | 61.5 | 54.1 |
| (b) Criteria for dividing Mobiltown into groups: | | | | | | | |
| Newtown/Oldtown | 19.1 | 16.7 | 25.9 | 24.1 | 33.3 | 35.5 | 36.6 |
| Newcomers/veterans | 33.5 | 23.3 | 20.4 | 12.0 | 18.8 | 44.0 | 7.2 |
| Other criteria | 47.4 | 60.0 | 53.7 | 63.9 | 47.9 | 20.5 | 56.2 |
| (N=512) | 100.0% | 100.0% | 100.0% | 100.0% | 100.0% | 100.0% | 100.0% |
| (c) Percentage agreeing: Different groups exist in Newtown (N=465) | 55.1 | 53.3 | 69.8 | 31.0 | 27.5 | 37.4 | 31.6 |
| (d) Percentage agreeing: Different groups exist in Oldtown (N=455) | 42.3 | 18.5 | 45.2 | 20.4 | 27.3 | 13.9 | 26.0 |

others point to age, moral standards, or politics as dividing criteria. It should be noted that the criteria that guided our study—neighborhood and seniority in Mobiltown—were most frequently mentioned. Specifically, the Newtown-Oldtown division was endorsed by a substantial portion of the respondents in all neighborhood groups. It was mentioned by MILIT and CIVILNEW somewhat less frequently than by the others.

When we consider period of residence and residential quarters together, the percentage of those who mention both criteria rises to about 80 percent of POORNEW, and it varies between 35 percent in Midtown to 53 percent of MILIT. Thus these are the major criteria in Mobiltown's self-image as a divided community. The importance of these criteria may be a result of their overlapping with other differential group attributes. Yet, the prominence of the division into residential quarters and seniority categories clearly supports our assumption of the importance of neighborhood groups as genuine status groups in Mobiltown.

To what extent do these perceptions of cleavages within the town describe a bluntly polarized reality or merely wider divisions made of more subtle differentiations? To answer this question, we must keep in mind that the more the images of social divisions are abrupt, unambiguous, and dichotomous, the more they reflect a conflictual understanding of the social order (Lockwood, 1966; Katznelson and Zolberg, 1986; Colbjornsen, 1988). An analysis of the perceptions of the division in Newtown and in Oldtown thus serves the evaluation of the understanding of the social order.

Table 5.1 (part c) shows that Oldtowners strongly share a view of Newtown as homogeneous. This view contrasts with the Newtowners' image of themselves, which emphasizes inner divisions. The military-civilian and new-veteran divisions in Newtown are perceived quite sharply by the quarters' own inhabitants. This is especially true of CIVILVET, which originates from Oldtown but now constitutes a minority of veterans in their new area of residence.

There is greater agreement between the inhabitants of the different neighborhood groups when it comes to perceptions of Oldtown. As part d of Table 5.1 shows, a majority of all groups view this part of the town as a single group. This view is shared by new residents and veterans and prevails among Poortowners, Midtowners, and Newtowners. Among them, MILIT and CIVILVET are relatively more inclined to point to the existence of different groups in Oldtown. These two groups may be aware of status differences in Oldtown for different reasons—CIVILVET as a group of mobile veterans and MILIT due to its group preparation for settling in Mobiltown.

Consideration of divisions both between and within neighborhoods reveals a deep consciousness throughout Mobiltown of differentiation within the community. This perception tends to be conflictual as it reveals a picture of clear-cut dichotomy. The Oldtowners are those who express the sharpest feelings—although indirectly—in this respect. They tend more than others to view both the Newtowners and themselves as "whole blocs." The group that appears to share the most elaborate understanding of the community consists of those mobile veterans who have detached themselves from Oldtown and moved into Newtown.

## PROFILES OF SOCIAL BOUNDARIES

The findings, then, reveal significant differences among the groups of Mobiltown in their perceptions of social boundaries in town. Are these differences consistent, thus reflecting general polarization within the town? In order to examine this issue, we performed a discriminant analysis of the major items referring to cleavages among Mobiltowners. The first significant function resulting from the analysis is presented in Table 5.2.

**Table 5.2**
**Discriminant Analysis: Identification of Groups in Mobiltown**
**(N=236)**

| Discriminating Variables and Standardized Discriminant Coefficients | Function 1 |
|---|---|
| Mobiltown divided into different groups* | -.31 |
| Mobiltown divided into Newtown/ Oldtown* | .00 |
| Mobiltown divided into newcomers/ veterans* | .84 |
| Different groups exist in Newtown* | .45 |
| Different groups exist in Oldtown* | -.00 |
| Canonical Correlation | .35 |
| Wilks' Lambda | .79 |
| p ($x^2$ test) | <.005 |
| **Group Centroids** | |
| MILIT | .56 |
| CIVILNEW | .21 |
| CIVILVET | .33 |
| MIDNEW | -.15 |
| MIDVET | -.19 |
| POORNEW | .25 |
| POORVET | -.40 |

* Dummy variable: the category defined in the table is coded 1; otherwise 0.

The function is relatively strong considering that we are dealing with perceptions of boundaries. The main differentiating items are "veteran versus new residents" and "the existence of different groups in Newtown." Thus, the neighborhood groups differ from each other mainly in their perceptions of social distribution by seniority in Mobiltown.

As the group centroids show, the neighborhood groups most aware of this distinction are those of Newtown, especially MILIT. It may be said, then, that the polarization is not uniform; it does not apply to the same extent to all possible criteria of social distinction nor to all neighborhood groups.

## IMAGES OF UNEQUAL POWER

It may now be asked, What is the nature of the relations that bind these groups to the community, and what position does each of them hold in the network they form?

In fact, a majority in all groups does share a view according to which "some groups in Mobiltown obtain more than others." This view is less pronounced in MILIT and CIVILNEW than among the other groups, as illustrated in Table 5.3: Newtowners are perceived by Oldtowners as the most powerful group in town while the former are more reluctant to claim that they hold such a position. Moreover, numerous Oldtowners do not differentiate between MILIT and CIVILNEW in this respect, while MILIT's neighbors, CIVILNEW and CIVILVET, are more prone to emphasize the relative advantage and privilege of MILIT.

Additional findings in Table 5.3 (part c) underline the significance of these conclusions. Powerlessness and deprivation are decried by a majority in almost all groups outside Newtown—with the sole exception of MIDNEW, where those who accept this stand fall just short of the majority. As might have been expected, a sense of powerlessness is especially prevalent in Poortown, where it is expressed by about two-thirds of the residents. It is least pronounced, of course, among Newtowners.

Consistent with these findings, Mobiltowners are divided with respect to their images of the degree and efficiency of the social mobilization of their groups. As part d of Table 5.3 shows, a majority of two-thirds among both POORNEW and POORVET depict their groups as unorganized and unsuccessful in obtaining their particular demands. In Midtown, a larger minority

**Table 5.3**
**Perceptions of Inter-Group Power Relations**

| | MILIT | CIVILNEW | CIVILVET | MIDNEW | MIDVET | POORNEW | POORVET |
|---|---|---|---|---|---|---|---|
| (a) Percentage agreeing: | | | | | | | |
| Some groups in town obtain more than others (N=479) | 57.3 | 65.2 | 74.4 | 67.7 | 74.0 | 90.6 | 77.4 |
| (b) Percentage agreeing: | | | | | | | |
| MILIT obtains more than its due share | 42.5 | 75.0 | 86.4 | 45.5 | 43.1 | 43.8 | 41.8 |
| All Newtowners obtain more than others (N=505) | 38.3 | 15.0 | 10.8 | 51.5 | 55.2 | 47.4 | 43.2 |
| (c) Percentage agreeing: | | | | | | | |
| One's own group is deprived compared with others (N=535) | 19.4 | 27.1 | 15.2 | 44.6 | 51.6 | 68.6 | 66.2 |
| (d) Percentage agreeing: | | | | | | | |
| One's own group is organized and successful | 56.5 | 21.7 | 40.5 | 15.9 | 16.7 | 5.6 | 8.9 |
| One's own group is organized and unsuccessful | 32.6 | 47.9 | 40.4 | 23.8 | 21.4 | 27.8 | 25.5 |
| One's own group is unorganized and unsuccessful | 10.9 | 30.4 | 19.1 | 58.7 | 61.9 | 66.6 | 65.6 |
| Total (N=527) | 100.0 | 100.0 | 100.0 | 100.0 | 100.0 | 100.0 | 100.0 |

acknowledges the social mobilization of their group, and about one-sixth even refers to successful lobbying. In Newtown, the majority of all groups notes the strength of their groups and describes them as successfully organized. MILIT appears to be the most self-confident in this respect.

These findings leave no doubt regarding the power configuration crystallizing in the minds of Mobiltowners, as an outcome of the demographic revolution experienced by the town. The new groups that were economically strong enough to settle in Newtown have actually become—at least in the eyes of Mobiltowners—the powerful stratum of the community. The other categories of Mobiltowners are more diffident than the Newtowners and express feelings of deprivation. Here again, however, CIVILVET emerges as the exception. While they belong to the veteran Mobiltowners, they are much closer to MILIT and CIVILNEW than to the Oldtowners in the images they share about their relative power in the town.

## PREJUDICES AND STEREOTYPES

Power perceptions differentiate groups from each other; they raise the issue of intergroup value judgments and the question of whether these perceptions lead to reciprocal hostility. We wanted to know to what extent the groups in Mobiltown have developed stereotypes about each other and whether they reject the labels attached to them by other groups.

Within the context of labeling patterns characteristic of Israel's group relations in general, we checked two specific Hebrew phrases that usually refer to definite and relevant categories—*merim et ha'af* and *zakuk le-tipuah tarbuti*. The first expression means "looks down on others," and it is generally used as a form of stigmatizing the "snobbish" well-to-do. The second label signifies "in need of cultural improvement," and refers to the poorly educated of inferior status.

It may be suggested that the more the different groups in Mobiltown use such stereotypes to depict each other, the more

**Table 5.4**
**Stereotypes in Mobiltown**

| | MILIT | CIVILNEW | CIVILVET | MIDNEW | MIDVET | POORNEW | POORVET |
|---|---|---|---|---|---|---|---|
| Percentage agreeing: There are groups in town who: | | | | | | | |
| (a) look down upon others (N=534) | 42.0 | 59.5 | 73.8 | 62.1 | 63.9 | 65.8 | 68.0 |
| (b) need cultural improvement (N=543) | 87.0 | 95.5 | 91.1 | 82.1 | 74.8 | 97.3 | 83.9 |

they are inclined to perceive clear-cut collective boundaries. Moreover, the more resolutely a group rejects the label used by others to describe it, the more hostile the intergroup relations with it.

Table 5.4 reveals an image that is both complex and interesting. For both statements, we found that compliance was dominant among the stigmatizer as well as the stigmatized in all groups. The first statement was strongly endorsed in reference to MILIT by all groups, including MILIT itself, albeit to a lesser extent. This suggests that for many of the military families in Newtown—as well as for Newtowners in general—to look down on others is considered legitimate behavior.

General agreement with the second statement was even stronger. A wide majority in all the groups agree that some groups in the community are "in need of cultural improvement"; this generalization includes the Poortowners, who are the principal target of this stereotype. This finding might be interpreted as expressing a passive internalization of their image. A more instrumental view might suggest that to be defined as "culturally deprived," in a welfare state like Israel, entitles one to privileges such as special educational facilities, housing rights, or welfare money, and therefore this label may be perceived as advantageous by the beneficiaries.

It thus appears that prejudice contributes to the clarification of social boundaries and to reciprocal negative images in Mobiltown. They do not necessarily, however, irritate relations between the groups.

## ATTITUDES TOWARD SOCIAL INTEGRATION

In such a context, to what extent do people of diverse social strata, ethnic origins, and seniority in town develop an effective collaboration? Do they succeed in "coexisting" and in developing forms of association in the various areas of social life?

**Table 5.5**
**Attitudes Toward Social Integration**

| | MILIT | CIVILNEW | CIVILVET | MIDNEW | MIDVET | POORNEW | POORVET |
|---|---|---|---|---|---|---|---|
| (a) Percentage agreeing: New and veteran groups cooperate in Mobiltown (N=528) | 49.5 | 39.1 | 67.5 | 28.7 | 32.9 | 34.2 | 33.1 |
| (b) Percentage agreeing: The settling of newcomers in Newtown has been beneficial for the town's: | | | | | | | |
| Municipal-technical services (N=566) | 46.9 | 33.3 | 34.8 | 16.0 | 35.9 | 28.9 | 31.7 |
| Education (N=569) | 70.7 | 60.4 | 57.4 | 44.0 | 58.8 | 43.6 | 53.4 |
| Community activities (N=566) | 57.1 | 59.6 | 44.6 | 45.4 | 41.1 | 47.4 | 42.7 |
| Political life (N=559) | 25.7 | 32.6 | 14.9 | 18.9 | 23.3 | 26.3 | 18.4 |

We asked our respondents to give their opinion on this statement: In Mobiltown new and veteran groups cooperate for the town's progress. Table 5.5 (part a) shows that no group supports this statement strongly. In all but two groups the majority of responses were negative. The more optimistic results come from MILIT and CIVILVET, the stronger groups.

This moderate estimation of factual integration leaves room for more positive responses when the questions become more specific and address the contribution of the project to areas such as the quality of education in the community or public activity in Mobiltown. The feelings about local politics and municipal services remain very reserved in all groups.

A closer look at the findings reveals additional interesting points. The stronger groups—MILIT, CIVILVET, and CIVILNEW—are the most satisfied. In general, the Oldtowner groups differ only slightly from one another in these respects, while differences between Newtowners are more noticeable. For instance, CIVILVET is less satisfied with the effects of integration on the realm of political life, probably because of the potential political threat of MILIT and CIVILNEW to its own power.

## CONCLUSION: LIVING WITH DISCREPANCIES

The major question we posed in this chapter is related to the subjective perceptions of the various neighborhood groups. Do their perceptions of themselves and their attitudes toward each other reflect their status group positions? That is, do they have distinct self-perceptions and view each other from a conflict perspective? Or do they, to the contrary, hold more egalitarian views of themselves and others in the community, thus reflecting the predictions of the contact hypothesis?

Most of our findings do not sustain the expectations of the contact hypothesis. Undoubtedly, the Mobiltown setting of intergroup contacts is more balanced than many other patterns that bring together stronger and weaker groups. In Mobiltown the better-off represent a minority that settled in a community where a local elite maintains its control over their integration. However, even here, the various groups still draw clear social boundaries and view their collaboration with reserve.

More than anything else, these groups know that they differ from each other in their power within the community, in the extent to which they share a lifestyle, and in the degree of their social cohesion. Subsequently, they are deeply aware of the inequality among them with respect to the benefits each group may extract from intergroup contact and cooperation. The stereotypic labels they attach to themselves and to other groups are asymmetric: all groups agree on defining the snobbish groups versus those that are "in need of cultural improvement." Thus, their perceptions reflect their distinct status group positions. The various neighborhood groups have developed an awareness of the divisions separating them and consequently emphasize the distances among themselves. They endorse cooperation only to a given degree and in specific areas. The "settle with us" project has fallen short of suppressing inequality, which, in fact, it never professed to abolish.

Our findings indicate that Mobiltown experiences an inequality that constitutes a potential for conflict. Yet Mobiltown has created the circumstances to live with this reality. The original ideology, it is true, was much more ambitious than the present one, and the real images of the community clearly illustrate a tendency toward polarization. However, most Mobiltowners feel that the practical experience is beneficial in specific respects.

The Mobiltown model has also created new inequalities and amplified existing ones. When we look at the various groups investigated, we see clear indications of differentiation within both the veteran and the new population of Mobiltown. The Mobiltowners constituted a fairly homogeneous community before the start of the project. Though social gaps between Poortowners and Midtowners existed prior to the "settle with us" project, we may reasonably assume that the effects of these gaps were less pronounced than today. On the basis of our findings, we suggest that the settling of new groups of higher social status may have encouraged social differentiation within the veteran population. Poortown is now characterized by sharp feelings of deprivation, self-images of weakness, and inability to organize and promote its particular interests. Poortowners are supportive of the project and believe that it has improved their condition. However, their feelings and perceptions make them a potential conflict group.

At the other end of the social spectrum of veteran Mobiltowners stands CIVILVET. This group is special in many respects. It is the most conscious of the social differentiations in both Newtown and Oldtown, and it strongly supports integration. It resents the power of MILIT and accuses those who "look down on others," but it does not view itself as deprived, and it aspires to maintain its power. CIVILVET is the best supporter of the Mobiltown project, although it is the least optimistic about the project's eventual political outcomes.

Actually, this group has undergone the greatest change in its life conditions as a result of the project. It has moved from its former environment to a new neighborhood. Here, however, it has become a "social minority," even though it includes most of the town's political leadership.

Another major actor in the social reality created by the Mobiltown project is MILIT. MILIT feels sure of its power, but it does not emphasize it bluntly. This may reflect the integrative ideology, or it can be understood as a politically profitable understatement. MILIT also holds images of fellow Mobiltowners that reflect negative attitudes. It particularly agrees that there are groups that are "in need of cultural improvement." At the same time, MILIT takes advantage of those services allocated on an integrative basis and declares itself fully supportive of the social philosophy behind the project.

In sum, each neighborhood group exhibits distinct attitudes and self- perceptions that correspond to its position as a status group. We saw earlier that objective status attributes, such as socioeconomic status, lifestyles, and friendship patterns, are efficient group markers in Mobiltown. We have seen here that the status group distinctions are also revealed in subjective domains, such as attitudes, outlooks, and proclaimed interests. The settlement project of Mobiltown has resulted in a great variety of collective images throughout the community. This divergence holds the potential of both conflict and cooperation.

# 6

# The Political Dimension: Elitism Versus Pluralism in the Community

The political scene in Mobiltown and its development are another major dimension of the meaning of the "settle with us" project. Do the different neighborhood groups find a way to collaborate, or do they oppose and confront one another? Do they create loose and changing coalitions, or do they develop permanent and rigid cleavages?

From a theoretical perspective, we may expect the political life of Mobiltown to develop in one of two directions, reflecting two contradicting models of political power: the elitist model versus the pluralist one. Since our analysis at this stage relates to the first years of the "settle with us" project, we do not expect the new and prestigious neighborhood groups to take control over Mobiltown's politics at this point. However, the two models reflect different ways in which the existing political leadership may relate to the newcomers.

The elitist model of community politics (Mills, 1956; Daalder, 1966; Badie and Birnbaum, 1983) asserts that ultimate power over a community is held by those who enjoy public preeminence. This power elite is assumed to rule according to its interests and outlooks. The democratic game, from this viewpoint, is simply an arena from which the elite draws support and obtains public recognition and legitimacy. This elite knows how to co-opt new elements that attain independent positions of prestige and power, in order to prevent them from becoming a political threat.

In Mobiltown, the power elite consists of the veteran political leadership. This leadership will sustain its elite position only if it succeeds in co-opting the newcomers and accommodating their demands within the existing political framework. In the long run, the elitist model predicts a conflict between the veteran leadership and the newcomers over the position of the community's power elite. Since the newcomers have established prestigious status groups, they will, according to the elitist model, enter into political struggle for control of the community.

In contrast to this model, the pluralistic model (Dahl, 1961; Frank and Dobson, 1985; Wooton, 1985) contends that the democratic game ensures that the political leadership does not become a political elite; the existence of various interest groups in the community draws the political leadership into a give-and-take situation, in which it succumbs to different political demands according to the changing circumstances. In addition, prestigious status groups are not necessarily regarded as aspiring to overtake power positions. They are not necessarily unified and may not even be interested in assuming public responsibility. Rather, they are interested in fulfilling their fragmented group interests. As a result, the political leadership is vulnerable to pressures exerted by those interest groups that are able to organize and make demands.

In Mobiltown, the pluralistic model would mean that the local leadership has nothing to be afraid of. The military officers and prosperous middle class that they invited to settle in Mobiltown should be principally interested in their own careers and welfare and remain largely detached from the problems of the community. At most, these groups should evolve as pressure groups that exert influence on those services that have direct impact on their well-being, such as education, cultural centers, and sports facilities. Outside the core of professional politicians, the political arena should thus be characterized mainly by the presence of various kinds of pressure groups.

We examine which of the two models of political power is more prominent in Mobiltown by focusing first on the political perceptions of the neighborhood groups regarding the issue of who rules Mobiltown. We then add our findings from observations and interviews regarding political life in the community.

## WHO RULES MOBILTOWN?

Our findings show that in the minds of the Mobiltowners not every group shares the same amount of power.

Table 6.1 (part a) shows that numerous respondents in all neighborhood groups state that the veteran and the new residents share the power. This view obtains the strongest support in no less than six of our seven groups. Among those who depict a more polarized political situation, the veterans are more often perceived as politically dominant. This is true in five out of the seven groups. The exception here is Poortown—especially POORNEW but also POORVET—who are more prone to point to MILIT and CIVILNEW as the dominant group in town. The reason for this particular attitude probably lies in the feelings of deprivation of these underprivileged groups, which are intensified by their exposure to the luxurious living conditions in Newtown. In this context, one easily generalizes from inequality in living conditions to politics and develops a dominant-subordinate view of the community. This may be especially so if the municipality, in order to make a success of the "settle with us" project or in response to pressures and lobbying, invests special efforts in Newtown.

Although the majority of respondents believe that the veterans dominate the town, this view is not of the same significance for all. When, for instance, CIVILVET endorses this stand, it actually refers to itself as the dominant group; when MILIT and CIVILNEW indicate the veterans as the "rulers," they refer to a category that does not include them. MILIT and CIVILNEW, then, appear to feel a lack of power. These findings are surprising: even though MILIT and CIVILNEW are newcomers in Mobiltown, they comprise senior military officers and wealthy

**Table 6.1**
**Perceptions of Political Life in Mobiltown**

| | MILIT | CIVILNEW | CIVILVET | MIDNEW | MIDVET | POORNEW | POORVET |
|---|---|---|---|---|---|---|---|
| (a) Who rules Mobiltown today? | | | | | | | |
| 1. Mainly the veterans | 32.6 | 33.3 | 31.1 | 30.8 | 26.0 | 13.9 | 21.0 |
| 2. Mainly the newcomers | 15.1 | 24.4 | 11.1 | 24.6 | 21.9 | 44.4 | 27.0 |
| 3. Veterans and newcomers together | 52.3 | 48.2 | 56.5 | 44.6 | 52.1 | 41.7 | 52.0 |
| Total (N=526) | 100.0% | 100.0% | 100.0% | 100.0% | 100.0% | 100.0% | 100.0% |
| (b) Who will rule Mobiltown in five years? | | | | | | | |
| 1. Mainly the veterans | 3.2 | 2.3 | 9.1 | 9.2 | 16.1 | 5.7 | 9.7 |
| 2. Mainly the newcomers | 53.7 | 31.8 | 45.5 | 53.8 | 37.6 | 45.7 | 47.6 |
| 3. Veterans and newcomers together | 43.2 | 65.9 | 45.5 | 36.9 | 46.2 | 48.6 | 42.8 |
| Total (N=521) | 100.0% | 100.0% | 100.0% | 100.0% | 100.0% | 100.0% | 100.0% |
| (c) Who will rule Mobiltown in 10 years? | | | | | | | |
| 1. Mainly the veterans | 2.2 | .0 | 7.1 | 3.1 | 11.6 | .0 | 4.1 |
| 2. Mainly the newcomers | 58.4 | 27.9 | 47.6 | 57.8 | 32.6 | 41.2 | 41.4 |
| 3. Veterans and newcomers together | 38.9 | 71.1 | 45.2 | 39.1 | 55.8 | 58.8 | 54.5 |
| Total (N=520) | 100.0% | 100.0% | 100.0% | 100.0% | 100.0% | 100.0% | 100.0% |

middle class, while the leaders are of local and underprivileged origin.

This apparent paradox is somewhat moderated by the findings shown in part b of Table 6.1, referring to images of Mobiltown's power relations in the future. When asked what they expect to be the case in five years, many of our respondents still appear to share integrative images. However, a weakening of these integrative prospects is noticeable.

More drastic changes are expected by those who deviate from the integrative view. The veterans are depicted as dominant by only a minority—and in most groups a small one—in all neighborhood groups. This includes CIVILVET, which includes many of the present leaders of Mobiltown. Instead, the new inhabitants of Newtown—MILIT and CIVILNEW—are viewed by much larger proportions of all groups as the future dominant stock. This perception is shared by a majority, or nearly a majority, in five out of our seven neighborhood groups. MILIT itself exhibits the strongest conviction in this respect; CIVILVET is also convinced that the newcomers will rule Mobiltown in the near future.

Here we find the explanation of earlier findings that the leading stratum of Mobiltown views the political impact of the "settle with us" project as a mixed blessing. MILIT and CIVILNEW are able to emphasize their positive contribution to Mobiltown's political life, notwithstanding their feelings of relative present weakness. These conclusions are further strengthened by the answers to a similar question referring to 10 years ahead. As Table 6.1 (part c) shows, the same general tendencies appear. MILIT exhibits an even stronger belief in Newtown's future strength, and the responses reflect an expectation that the veteran leadership will lose some of its influence.

The latter findings may be better understood in light of Mobiltown's present political situation and the present image of the local leadership. Table 6.2 (part a) shows that for a large portion of the population, these leaders are representative of the community as a whole. However, in each neighborhood group, with the only and understandable exception of CIVILVET, a

**Table 6.2**
**Whom Does Mobiltown's Leadership Represent?**

| | MILIT | CIVILNEW | CIVILVET | MIDNEW | MIDVET | POORNEW | POORVET |
|---|---|---|---|---|---|---|---|
| (a) Whom do Mobiltown's leaders represent? | | | | | | | |
| 1. Their own group | 43.0 | 35.7 | 11.4 | 42.0 | 34.7 | 40.5 | 34.0 |
| 2. Other groups | 2.3 | 2.4 | .0 | 2.9 | 2.0 | .0 | 3.3 |
| 3. Mobiltown in general | 33.7 | 52.4 | 72.7 | 44.9 | 44.9 | 27.0 | 42.0 |
| 4. Themselves | 20.9 | 9.5 | 15.9 | 10.1 | 18.4 | 32.4 | 15.9 |
| Total (N=526) | 100.0% | 100.0% | 100.0% | 100.0% | 100.0% | 100.0% | 100.0% |
| (b) Do Mobiltown's leaders represent you? | | | | | | | |
| 1. Yes, to a large extent | 12.4 | 10.4 | 26.7 | 10.0 | 12.7 | 7.9 | 5.2 |
| 2. To some extent | 51.4 | 77.1 | 48.4 | 47.1 | 40.2 | 39.5 | 42.2 |
| 3. No | 36.0 | 12.5 | 24.4 | 42.9 | 47.1 | 52.6 | 52.6 |
| Total (N=546) | 100.0% | 100.0% | 100.0% | 100.0% | 100.0% | 100.0% | 100.0% |

majority or nearly a majority do not believe that the leaders represent their group. Conspicuously, these leaders are viewed by many as committed mainly to the members of their own group or even to themselves.

The feeling that the leadership represents primarily its own stock—the veteran population—is particularly strong among the new groups of residents throughout Mobiltown (POORNEW, MIDNEW, and MILIT, with CIVILNEW and POORVET slightly behind them). This undoubtedly expresses some alienation from Mobiltown's leadership on the part of the entire new population of the town. Two of the veteran groups (POORVET and CIVILVET) and CIVILNEW, CIVILVET's immediate neighbors, see these leaders as representative of the community as a whole. On the other hand, as a group, Poortowners seem to be the most suspicious of the leaders; they have the greatest tendency to depict the leaders as motivated by their personal interests.

Consistent with the above findings, many of the respondents do not consider the present leadership as widely representing their group. This is clearly demonstrated by Table 6.2. CIVILVET is the only group in which more than a quarter of the respondents share a categorically positive attitude in this respect. At the other end, Poortown demonstrates the sharpest alienation from the local leaders, with more than half of the respondents feeling totally unrepresented by them. It is also interesting that Midtown is slightly less favorable toward the leaders than MILIT or CIVILNEW. These findings indicate a gap between the leadership and almost all segments of the community. This gap explains why the leadership feels threatened by the potential power represented by the new inhabitants of Newtown.

## MOBILTOWN'S POLITICAL ELITE

In order to comprehend fully the political situation of the present elite in Mobiltown, we further examine its origins and its patterns of ruling the town. The dominant party in Mobiltown has been the right-wing LIKUD ever since "the youngsters," headed by the charismatic and dominant figure of M., succeeded in taking over the party branch in Mobiltown, and gained control of the municipal council.

The new clique actually ran the town without investing much in the party itself, which remained a loose and unarticulated structure. M. was the one to make all the decisions after consulting his entourage, which includes several members of his family.

We conducted numerous in-depth interviews with 34 activists, politicians, and public servants during a period of several months (from November 1986 to July 1987). At the same time, we questioned Mobiltowners from all social strata in order to get a detailed picture of the community's public life.

During that period, the leader, M., handed the mayoralty over to the deputy mayor. This caused a genuine shock throughout the town. M. had been the initiator and leader of Mobiltown's upward mobility, and his power in the town was at its peak. Heading a community that had been transformed, he also became one of the prominent younger leaders of the LIKUD; he was elected to the Knesset (the Israeli parliament) and began pursuing a political career at the national level.

Leaving Mobiltown's town council at this time could also be considered a wise political calculation. A degradation in M.'s status among the Mobiltowners themselves would have soon been inevitable due to the severe difficulties that arose from the project. The local politicians coped with these emerging difficulties according to the patterns that have always been typical of Mobiltown. These are characterized by the existence of cliques, unofficial coalitions of kinship networks, and allegiances grounded in individual interests. This was so widely accepted that a member of M.'s entourage unabashedly told us, "M. is so strong in town that he is capable of determining any key nomination in any public service, even if there are special appointment committees."

This style of political life was not considered unfair, nor did it raise any serious objection as long as Mobiltown was a widely homogeneous, low-class Mizrachi town easily controlled by its leadership. However, once the senior military officers, professionals, and other middle-class people representing the main stream of Israeli society had settled there, strong criticism began to be heard. M. was now often called the "sheriff of Mobiltown."

To gain authority over these newcomers, whom he himself had brought to the town, M. co-opted several Newtowners who showed special interest in politics. Ironically, these were tactics learned from the Israeli establishment, which used them during the 1950s with North African and Middle Eastern Jewish immigrants. In the very same way, the second generation of those immigrants in Mobiltown nominated Newtowners—many of them Ashkenazim—to positions such as the director of the town's planning division, members of the board of education, secretary general of the municipality, and the editor of the local newspaper. The municipality also made more or less open concessions to Newtown in various areas of public services ranging from increasing the frequency of garbage collection to supporting a restrictive admission policy at Newtown's local country club.

The town's leaders also knew how to strengthen their relationship with other political forces—in particular the Labor party, their principal opposition. Tacit agreements were reached so as to prevent the newcomers from using existing political frameworks to take over the municipality.

The legitimation of the leadership was also a major goal. The 1987 celebration of Mobiltown's new status as a city—after the population reached 20,000—became a day of glory for M. A lengthy poem read at this ceremony presented Mobiltown's history as beginning with M.'s mayoralty and Mobiltown itself as his very personal creation.

Word has it in Mobiltown that M. handed over the municipality to his deputy, B., only after spending several nights dictating a whole volume of advice and directives. The group of local politicians formed by M. remained in power. They will have to face attempts by Newtowners to try their own chances in community politics. As a rule, these inhabitants of MILIT or CIVILNEW have higher formal education and status, and they are much more representative of Israel's dominant culture. M. and his clique, however, are much more politically astute. They know better how to manipulate support and power, and they weave their political prominence over those groups in a professional manner.

This situation is particularly complex since many of the new residents of Newtown are politically identified with the Labor party rather than with the ruling LIKUD. Therefore they shared an additional motivation actively to oppose Mobiltown's "regime."

Mobiltown's Labor party, in fact, had been in bad shape for many years. It had no public figure who could compare with M. and had no appeal to the veteran public, before the establishment of Newtown or after it. This is so despite the wide range of institutions that depend on this party and that operate in the community on a regular basis, such as the workers' council and the working women's council. The party was deeply divided into factions that paralyzed each other. Moreover, many veteran members of this party collaborated with the LIKUD in order to ensure their own position. M.'s power and that of his successors extended beyond the LIKUD circles, thanks to their domination of the municipal bureaucracy and their informal networks.

All these factors account for the reluctance of many Labor leaders to declare a war on the LIKUD's power. This reluctance was reinforced by the attempts of MILIT and CIVILNEW to achieve power. Among the latter, many aspired to conquer the local Labor party on their way to fighting the hegemony of the LIKUD and of M.'s friends and successors.

While one group of Newtowners tried in vain to gain control of the Labor party branch, another group was trying to set up a new local party for the municipal elections. This attempt also fell short of success and was broken down by the co-optative policy of the ruling group.

These circumstances, however, do not mean that Newtowners were unable to accumulate some political assets and to gain specific advantages within the community.

## FIGHTING FOR ASSETS

As a matter of fact, the inhabitants of Newtown have been quite active on the public scene. MILIT, especially, is well organized, and its action involves a variety of specific goals.

Most neighborhoods in Mobiltown elect a committee that represents them at the municipality. At the present time, MILIT's committee is by far the most powerful, as its population is the most united and in general endorses its decisions vigorously. Therefore this committee has been able to undertake important projects and to define a strategy in order to achieve specific advantages.

For example, MILIT's committee was able—in collaboration with that of the civilian Newtowners—to fight against a rise in municipal taxes on high-standard houses and apartments, to sponsor a sophisticated TV antenna system in the neighborhood, and to achieve better public transportation. In all these cases, petitions, lobbying officials, and repeated pressures on the mayor were successful.

These struggles for privileges did not prevent the Newtowners from fully participating in community feasts, educational events, and social gatherings organized by the municipality and intended to symbolize integration and cohesion among all Mobiltown's neighborhoods. At the same time, attending these events did not prevent MILIT from pursuing a policy aimed at emphasizing its distinction from other neighborhoods.

The best illustration of this duality is the so-called water park affair. The story starts with a sum of surplus money left over after the contractors completed construction of MILIT's homes. The neighborhood committee decided to use this balance of credit to build a park with a swimming pool and other country club facilities. However, it soon appeared that more money was necessary to complete the project. At the same time, the municipality was expressing reservations about a public project that would not be aimed at the community as a whole. For MILIT's committee, the difficult question was how to widen the project in such a way that for all practical purposes it would still be exclusively used by a restricted population. Months of negotiations with the municipality finally led to an agreement that allowed the committee to launch an offer to the public to join the club on the basis of a $1,000 membership fee. This, of course, drastically reduced the chances of most Mobiltowners to join.

MILIT's activity extended beyond its neighborhood committee; education was another area of interest. Newtown parents became deeply involved in school committees, and a large number of teachers were recruited from this neighborhood. As a result, conflicts emerged, in some instances involving the authorities of the school, the parents, the teachers, and the municipality.

One of the sharpest confrontations occurred in an elementary school of grades four to six. Half of the schoolchildren were from Newtown, and the parents' committee was chaired by a resident from MILIT. In fact, the neighborhood was eager to take control of the school's committee. Out of the 10 members of this committee, 6 were from MILIT, 3 from CIVILNEW, and only 1 from Poortown. Hostility between the committee and the school principal began with an incident between the latter and a pupil from MILIT, over a matter of discipline. The pupil's outraged father came to the school to complain vehemently about the child's punishment; the principal ousted him and registered a complaint with the police. At about the same time, the principal demanded that the ministry of education dismiss one of the teachers in the school whom he deemed unfit. This teacher also happened to be an inhabitant of MILIT. These incidents were sufficient impetus for the MILIT-dominated school committee to start a campaign to have the principal fired. At this point, rumors began circulating about financial mismanagement of the school.

This conflict continued for several months without any definite conclusion; a special "action committee" was created to organize petitions, strikes, and public protest. Unwilling to concede too easily to the pressures of the new population of Newtown, the municipality backed the principal. The principal himself rehired the dismissed teacher and tried to create a conciliatory atmosphere. One and a half years later, a change of principals finally took place, conclusively indicating the political strength of MILIT in the community.

The dynamic temper of MILIT is expressed in numerous other forms. We studied some of the committees that supervised the activities of Mobiltown's community center. One such committee is the Repertoire Committee, which is in charge of organizing artistic performances at the center every three or four weeks. This committee consisted of 10 to 15 members, about two-thirds of them inhabitants of Newtown—mostly MILIT. Typical middle-class people, they were generally inclined to order performances that responded to the taste of their own neighborhoods. When questioned, they rationalized their choices by emphasizing their "beneficial" role in the community in "raising its cultural level" and encouraging intergroup relations on the basis of "good taste." As we were told by one of the leading members of the committee: "We have no intention of responding to any demand; we are to meet given social and cultural standards of a high quality. It is on this ground that we want to attract the whole population of the town to the center."

Other activities of the center were more integrated. A good example is the Dancing Circle Club, which at the time of our research was particularly popular, with about 40 weekly participants. Here there was more contact between residents of the different neighborhoods, and, according to participants, these relations were very gratifying. Nevertheless, we were also told that once it became necessary to divide the circle between experienced and new dancers, this was done in a manner that widely coincided with the Newtown-Oldtown division. Here, too, we found that the club was run by several residents of MILIT, with some from CIVILNEW.

Another form of cultural activity is the Tsavta (Together) Club. This club was set up in Mobiltown after the establishment of Newtown, and all its organizers belonged to MILIT. The declared aim was to propagate "progressive culture," a term used for activities such as lectures on scientific, philosophical, and literary subjects, musical gatherings, recitals, poetry readings, and political debates. Tsavta is associated with the left-wing MAPAM party, and the leadership of the rightist LIKUD in Mobiltown was one of the reasons the new club had difficulties. In addition, the nature of its activities made this club an object of interest for only a small group of highly educated people, primarily residents of Newtown.

The organizers did at one time think of including activities in their program that could attract a wider audience (for instance, inviting popular performers), but they later dismissed this idea. Our inquiry also shows that publicity for the activities was, for the most part, limited to a restricted mailing list aimed mainly at Newtown. Posters advertising events were generally displayed in Newtown only. We saw about 20 to 30 persons at the gatherings that we attended, all but 3 or 4 of them Newtowners, and most of them inhabitants of MILIT. In sum, although Tsavta is far from a comprehensive framework for cultural life in Newtown, it does represent one more marker of the distinctiveness of this part of Mobiltown, focusing on quasi-exclusive participation.

The realm of sports does not constitute an "integrated aspect" of Mobiltown, either. We found five sports centers in the town, all but one situated in schools. Each of these centers offered a wide range of activities—from soccer and basketball to tennis, athletics, swimming, and karate. Our data reveal that here, too, clear differences distinguished Newtowners and Oldtowners, among both adults and children. For instance, soccer was of special importance in Mobiltown, as the town's team played in the top national league; this game was largely monopolized by Oldtown. On the other hand, adult sports, which are essentially leisure activities, mainly served Newtown, especially in the case of tennis, swimming, and athletics for both women and men.

As for children's sports, separation according to neighborhood groups was quite the rule. Even when various sports activities were offered in the same center, as is frequently the case, one finds most of Newtown's children in basketball, tennis, and gymnastics, and most of Oldtown's children in the martial arts or soccer. Even though the official policy of the town was to encourage integrative sports programs, different norms among the diverse groups of the population created the distinction.

More striking developments have taken place in the commercial life of the town. Up to the mid-1980s, there were only two commercial centers: an area of small and shabby shops typical of a poverty area and a weekly open market, where goods of all kinds were sold at cheap prices at dozens of stands. Soon after their arrival, the Newtowners pressured the municipality to allow the construction of a new commercial center that would better respond to their needs and economic standing. This new shopping center was set up in Newtown itself. The shops belong to proprietors from out of town or from Newtown, while most of the employees are from Oldtown and the customers come principally from MILIT, CIVILVET, or CIVILNEW. The weekly market continued to attract Mobiltowners from both parts of the town because of its low prices. However, while many Oldtowners remained loyal to their old commercial center—which also improved its appearance—the Newtowners now had the privilege of a high-standard center, with delicatessens, boutiques, and expensive restaurants. This center has become one more asset associated with the new inhabitants of Mobiltown and, above all, one more symbol of their distinction.

## CONCLUSIONS

The survey of Mobiltown's population reveals a paradox. The local elite has maintained its control of the municipality and has actually succeeded in implementing its ambitious settlement scheme and reaping the political benefits. The subsequent alienation, mainly in Poortown, is by no means a surprise.

What may seem less obvious is that the new strong groups—MILIT and CIVILNEW—have remained in a secondary position, despite the almost unanimous expectation that they will achieve predominance in the future.

The data show that the new inhabitants of Newtown—and especially MILIT—are the best organized and the most ambitious residents of Mobiltown. They have systematically attained important organizational assets in the community and are able to create new foci of activity that reflect their impact on the community in the realm of education, culture, sports, and commerce.

All these efforts, however, are not enough to ensure them central political power in the town. This cannot be explained by unwillingness or lack of interest on their part. The Newtowners have tried all sorts of tactics to become a powerful factor in Mobiltown's public scene. However, the experienced local politicians have known whom to co-opt and what to concede.

For the time being, Mobiltown portrays a political system that by and large illustrates the pluralist model. Though the local leaders invested efforts to co-opt the newcomers and maintain control of the power processes in Mobiltown, the strong groups of newcomers, especially MILIT, have been able to act as interest groups on their own behalf. These processes could actually have been expected. A status enhancement project, such as the one carried out in Mobiltown, creates new groups that form prestigious status groups. As such, they struggle to fulfill their group interests after settling in their new homes. It is very difficult for the veteran political leadership to co-opt them into the existing political framework without succumbing to their particular interests. At the first stage, therefore, a pluralist model of political struggle is revealed, in which the veteran leadership still maintains its power, while the new groups get their interests fulfilled.

The question is what will happen in the long run. The ability of the new groups to satisfy their interests provides them with power in the community. In the future, they may wish to transform this power base into actual political control of the community. As prestigious status groups, they may struggle to become the power elite of Mobiltown in the vein of the elitist model. The veteran leadership, being perceived as yielding to the newcomers' interests, may enter this struggle in a disadvantaged position. It is thus likely that the current pluralist model of Mobiltown's politics will turn into an elitist one. The perceptions of the Mobiltowners regarding the future "rulers" of Mobiltown point to such a possibility.

# 7

# School Integration and the Young Generation

In the long run, the success of the Mobiltown experiment depends on the way the younger generation in town perceives the reality in which they are brought up. In this chapter we focus on the young generation of Mobiltowners, namely, the students in the elementary, junior high, and high schools of Mobiltown. Since the schools on all three levels include students from both new and veteran neighborhoods, our focus on the students carries a double significance. First, it enables us to see how the youngsters of Mobiltown, as compared with their parents, view the sociodemographic changes in their own town, at least to the extent that these changes are reflected in school life on different school levels. The major part of the chapter thus consists of the analysis of data collected in a separate students' survey and focusing on the students' perceptions. We ask how students of the different neighborhood groups view themselves, how they view the groups of new versus veteran students, and how they perceive the coexistence between these groups. More important, we examine the extent to which these perceptions are directly influenced by the neighborhood group affiliation of the students. Since we are concerned with youngsters, these analyses may enable us to get a glimpse at the future coexistence of new and veteran neighborhood groups in Mobiltown.

However, the focus on school students also carries a second significance, related to the present situation in Mobiltown. Contrary to other social and communal frameworks, where the meeting between new and veteran residents is mostly voluntary, the school imposes at least some sort of mutual relations among students of different neighborhood groups. Being in school, the students are actually involved in the single compulsory meeting ground among members of the various neighborhood groups. The students' perceptions regarding themselves and other students are therefore crucial for evaluating the total picture of intergroup relations in Mobiltown, since they are based on the daily mutual experiences of youngsters from various neighborhood groups.

With regard to the current perceptions of the students and the implications of these perceptions for Mobiltown's future, we rely on the general theoretical framework of our study. Thus, our aim is to find whether the imposed contact among students of the various neighborhood groups results in feelings of superiority, deprivation, and antagonism or whether it leads to positive attitudes of all students involved in the contact. In either case, the students' attitudes are also taken to indicate the future direction of conflict versus integration among Mobiltown's neighborhood groups.

## INTEGRATION OF THE SCHOOL SYSTEM AND PARENTS' VIEWS

The political leaders of Mobiltown were well aware of the significance of the school system as a meeting ground between Newtown and Oldtown. From the early days of Newtown's planning they put an emphasis on the integration of the new settlers into the existing school system and declared this to be a goal of the "settle with us" project.

Before the Newtowners' arrival, the school system already comprised several elementary schools (grades 1 to 6), two junior high schools (grades 7 to 9), and two comprehensive high schools (grades 10 to 12, including both academic and vocational tracks). At each school level, the schools were divided into secular state schools and religious state schools, the latter being smaller in size and less relevant for the integration of the new settlers, who are less traditional.

Due to the relatively young age of the newcomer families, the issue of school integration mainly involved the elementary school level. As Table 7.1 shows, the children of all three Newtown groups concentrate in either elementary school or in preschool ages. Preschool institutions, such as day-care centers or kindergartens, are neighborhood-based and do not raise the integration issue. As for the elementary schools, Mobiltown's leaders wanted, at first, to bus Newtown's children into Oldtown's schools. This plan, however, was not feasible, due to the large number of children involved and the opposition of the Newtowners, especially MILIT. The latter mobilized the support of the Ministry of Education for their own plan, which was finally accepted. Two new elementary schools, one for grades one to three, and the other for grades four to six, were built in Newtown, close to its border with Poortown. "Integration" was achieved by transferring the Poortown students to the new schools. This solution seemed satisfactory to all parties involved. While it prevented a full residential segregation of Newtown's elementary schools, Poortown's students constituted only a minority of the student population of the new schools.

With regard to secondary education, it was clear from the start that Newtown's youngsters would have to attend the schools already existing in Oldtown. In both the secular junior high school and the secular high school they constituted a substantial minority of the student population—a minority that, in general, demonstrated high academic achievements. The secondary schools decided to cope with the higher standards of the new students through their internal tracking mechanisms. Ability grouping in major study subjects—especially mathematics and English—is practiced in the junior high school, as well as in the higher grades of the elementary school. The secular high school established a new prestigious technology track, in addition to the existing vocational and academic tracks. This track leads to the attainment of the matriculation diploma, which is a prerequisite for university enrollment. Obviously, Newtown's students tend

**Table 7.1**
**Respondents Reporting Children of Preschool and School Age by Neighborhood Group**

| | MILIT | CIVILNEW | CIVILVET | MIDNEW | MIDVET | POORNEW | POORVET |
|---|---|---|---|---|---|---|---|
| Preschool children | 37.2 | 41.7 | 29.2 | 67.6 | 35.8 | 53.2 | 28.5 |
| Elementary school | 42.1 | 37.4 | 37.1 | 23.6 | 29.1 | 27.7 | 38.6 |
| Junior high school | 18.3 | 12.1 | 20.2 | 5.9 | 16.9 | 10.6 | 15.8 |
| High school | 2.4 | 8.8 | 13.5 | 2.9 | 18.2 | 8.5 | 17.1 |
| Total | 100.0% | 100.0% | 100.0% | 100.0% | 100.0% | 100.0% | 100.0% |
| N* | 164 | 91 | 89 | 68 | 148 | 47 | 158 |

* N is based on the number of respondents who reported having at least one child in each of the given preschool or school age groups.

**Table 7.2**
**Parents' Views of School Integration by Neighborhood Group**

| | MILIT | CIVILNEW | CIVILVET | MIDNEW | MIDVET | POORNEW | POORVET |
|---|---|---|---|---|---|---|---|
| (a) View About School Integration of Students from Different Social Groups: | | | | | | | |
| Too much emphasis on integration | 10.4 | 13.2 | 19.5 | 15.2 | 12.2 | 10.0 | 14.0 |
| Adequate emphasis | 59.7 | 55.3 | 56.1 | 54.5 | 63.5 | 40.0 | 43.9 |
| Inadequate emphasis | 29.9 | 31.5 | 24.4 | 30.3 | 24.3 | 50.0 | 42.1 |
| Total (N = 390) | 100.0% | 100.0% | 100.0% | 100.0% | 100.0% | 100.0% | 100.0% |
| (b) Influence of Co-existence of New and Veteran Neighborhoods on Education in Mobiltown: | | | | | | | |
| Bad influence | 6.5 | 8.7 | 8.6 | 12.5 | 16.3 | 10.6 | 18.2 |
| No influence | 18.3 | 28.3 | 34.0 | 35.9 | 22.4 | 44.7 | 22.4 |
| Good influence | 75.2 | 63.0 | 57.4 | 51.6 | 61.3 | 44.7 | 59.4 |
| Total (N = 529) | 100.0% | 100.0% | 100.0% | 100.0% | 100.0% | 100.0% | 100.0% |
| (c) Chance for Your Children to Succeed in School as Compared with Other Students of Their Age: | | | | | | | |
| Less chance | 0.0 | 0.0 | 6.7 | 1.8 | 7.2 | 5.7 | 17.5 |
| The same chance | 78.9 | 84.1 | 84.4 | 92.8 | 91.8 | 85.7 | 78.5 |
| A better chance | 21.1 | 15.9 | 8.9 | 5.4 | 1.0 | 8.6 | 4.0 |
| Total (N = 493) | 100.0% | 100.0% | 100.0% | 100.0% | 100.0% | 100.0% | 100.0% |

to be placed in the higher ability-groups and in the more prestigious tracks.

Put together, school integration in Mobiltown means that Newtowners and Oldtowners study in the same schools. Within each school, however, Newtown's students may enjoy better educational opportunities, according to their academic abilities.

Parents' views of school integration in Mobiltown may therefore vary by neighborhood group affiliation. In the general survey there were three items related to views of school integration. As Table 7.2 shows, the respondents from all neighborhood groups tend to agree that the emphasis on school integration in Mobiltown is "adequate," that is, has a good influence on the quality of education in town, and that their own children have the same chance to succeed in school as other students of their age. However, there are some interesting variations among several neighborhood groups. The contrast between MILIT and POORVET is especially illuminating. While MILIT parents are satisfied with school integration, contend that it positively influences education in Mobiltown, and yet tend to admit that their own children stand a better chance than others at school, those of POORVET claim that the emphasis on school integration is inadequate. A relatively high percentage of them contend that school integration has had a "bad" influence on education in Mobiltown and that their own children stand a lower chance at school than others. There seems to be a close relation between the general attitude of neighborhood groups toward school integration and the extent to which they believe their own children can benefit from this situation. This is further demonstrated by the response patterns of CIVILVET. More than any other group, these parents claim that there has been too much emphasis on school integration. They are less certain than MILIT or CIVILNEW that their children stand a better chance than others at school; this may indicate that their children's status in school was lowered by the influx of Newtown's students. Their reservations about school integration may well be an additional symptom of their position as the mobile group among the veteran residents.

## THE STUDENTS' SURVEY

More important than parents' views are the views of the students themselves, who are actually involved in school integration. How do they perceive the integration of new and veteran students? Are they aware of socioeconomic and academic differences between new and veteran students? Does this situation influence their self-image?

The key issues in these questions are the differences in perceptions between students of the new and students of the veteran neighborhood groups and the extent to which neighborhood group affiliation directly influences their perceptions. Ideally, successful school integration should lessen group differences in perceptions. As the general literature on school desegregation shows, this may depend on the egalitarianism in the encounter between students of the different groups.

Among the various factors that may affect status equality between the groups (Mercer, Iadicola, and Moore, 1986), three are most relevant to school integration in Mobiltown: equality of socioeconomic status, the political climate, and the treatment of the disadvantaged social group as "insiders." While there are large socioeconomic differences (and, hence, also differences in academic achievement) between new and veteran students in Mobiltown, the political climate, as we have seen, is generally supportive of school integration. In addition, the veteran students, who constitute the lower-status group, cannot be treated as "outsiders" by the new and higher-status students. Their longer residence in the community may even serve as a status resource and hence facilitate their contacts with the new students despite their socioeconomic differences. The issue of neighborhood group differences in students' perceptions is therefore especially intriguing in Mobiltown, where school integration is more complex and quite different from regular situations of school desegregation.

In order to examine this issue, we conducted a separate students' survey. It consisted of closed-item questionnaires, which were self-administered in the classrooms by all students of the secular high school and the secular junior high school and by students of the highest (sixth) grade of the integrative elementary school in Newtown. Altogether, it was filled in by 755 students—109 of the elementary school, 389 of the junior high, and 257 of the high school. Among these, the percentages of students from the new neighborhood groups, MILIT and CIVILNEW, are 76 percent, 37 percent, and 50 percent, respectively.

Because of some small differences in attitudinal items and mainly because of differences in the internal grouping of students, the responses of the high school students were analyzed separately from those of the students in the junior high and the elementary schools. However, in all schools the survey focused mainly on three sets of students' perceptions, related to (1) the self-image of the students, (2) the integration of new and veteran students, and (3) the groups involved in the process. The exact items of each set are presented in Table 7.3. Here we briefly discuss each set and its underlying rationale.

### Self-image

The academic and social self-image of the students was measured by five items. School desegregation research has shown that lower-status students in heterogeneous settings have a lower self-image than students of a similar status in homogeneous settings (St. John, 1975). This is due to the tendency of the lower-status students to use the higher-status students as a reference group. Similar results were obtained in Israel (Arzi and Amir, 1976; Chen, Lewy, and Kfir, 1977). In our context, the questions are whether new students have a higher self-image than the veterans and to what extent their differences in self-perceptions are independently explained by neighborhood group affiliation.

### Perception of Integration

This set is composed of four items, measuring the perceived effects of mixing new and veteran students on the respondent personality and on classroom studying and relationships among classmates and with teachers. Previous studies indicate the strong influence of adult community members, particularly parents and teachers, on students' perceptions of school desegregation (Gerrard and Miller, 1975; Mercer et al., 1986). As the distributions of the four items in Table 7.3 indicate, the general support of school integration in Mobiltown is reflected in the students' responses. Of course, the question is whether students vary in their views of school integration according to their neighborhood groups.

### Perception of the Groups

This set pertains to the stereotypes of new and veteran students in four domains: academic success, social relationships, socioeconomic status, and chances of life success. The distributions show an average tendency to perceive the new students as superior to the veterans, especially with respect to academic standing and socioeconomic status. Most studies on group perception in desegregated settings reveal an asymmetrical pattern—both higher- and lower-status groups perceive the former as superior (see Mercer et al., 1986; and also Peres, 1976, and Schwarzwald and Amir, 1984, for Israeli findings). The question is whether a similar asymmetry will be found between students of the new and students of the veteran neighborhood groups, or if each group will use its own status resources (socioeconomic level, length of community residence) to form more symmetric group perceptions.

**Table 7.3**
**Description and Distribution of Perceptions among Mobiltown Students in Elementary and Junior High School (N=498) and in High School (N=257)**

| | | Elementary and Junior High School | | High School | |
|---|---|---|---|---|---|
| | | Mean | S.D. | Mean | S.D. |
| **Self-Perception (S)** | | | | | |
| S1 | Are you popular among your classmates? (1=not so much; 2=quite; 3=very much) | 2.16 | 0.56 | 2.26 | 0.49 |
| S2 | How would you define your academic success (1=a very weak student... 6=excellent) | 4.02 | 0.94 | 3.93 | 0.88 |
| S3 | Upon completion of junior high school do you intend to study (0= in the vocational track; 1=in the academic track) | 0.48 | 0.50 | - | - |
| S3 | Do you intend to pursue your studies after high school graduation? (1=no; 2=postsecondary studies; 3=university) | - | - | 2.41 | 0.75 |
| S4 | Do you think you will obtain a matriculation diploma? (0=no or maybe; 1=yes) | 0.54 | 0.50 | 0.73 | 0.23 |
| S5 | Do you have the same chance of life success as others of your age? (1=less chance; 2=the same; 3=better) | 2.04 | 0.39 | 2.12 | 0.42 |

| | | | | | |
|---|---|---|---|---|---|
| **Integration Perception (I)** | | | | | |
| | Students at your school are both veterans and new in Mobiltown. How does this fact influence the following? | | | | |
| I1 | Studying in the classroom (1=bad influence; 2=no influence; 3=good influence) | 2.23 | 0.61 | 2.41 | 0.65 |
| I2 | Relationships among classmates (1=bad influence; 2=no influence; 3=good influence) | 2.04 | 0.72 | 2.10 | 0.66 |
| I3 | Relationships with teachers (1=bad influence; 2=no influence; 3=good influence) | 2.08 | 0.56 | 2.10 | 0.50 |
| I4 | You personally (1=bad influence; 2=no influence; 3=good influence) | 2.24 | 0.59 | 2.18 | 0.57 |
| **Group Perception (G)** | | | | | |
| | Do the new and veteran students differ in: | | | | |
| G1 | Academic success? (1=veterans more successful; 2=same; 3=new more successful) | 2.48 | 0.54 | 2.49 | 0.52 |
| G2 | Relationships with other students? (1=veterans more sociable; 2=same; 3=new more sociable) | 2.17 | 0.63 | 1.97 | 0.55 |
| G3 | Parents' economic level? (1=veterans more affluent; 2=same; 3=new more affluent) | 2.44 | 0.53 | 2.55 | 0.51 |
| G4 | Life success chances? (1=veterans have better chances;2=same;3=new have better chances | 2.29 | 0.50 | 2.29 | 0.46 |

## STUDENTS' PERCEPTIONS BY NEIGHBORHOOD GROUPS

In order to examine differences by neighborhood groups in the students' perceptions, we performed discriminant analyses of the three perception sets separately for the elementary and junior high school students and for the high school students. Each analysis yielded a single significant discriminant function, which is presented in Table 7.4. In all the analyses, the perceptions were discriminated by five neighborhood group affiliations of the students: MILIT, CIVILNEW, CIVILVET, MIDTOWN, and POORTOWN. The last two categories consist mainly of veteran students. MIDNEW and POORNEW students, who were too few in number to form separate groups, were included in these categories.

As the table shows, the students' self-perceptions were best discriminated by group affiliation on both school levels. On both levels, the discrimination is attributed to academic self-image, particularly the perception of academic success at the elementary and junior high level, and the expectation to obtain a matriculation diploma at the high school level. The centroids show that the students are ordered by level of self-esteem in accordance with the status hierarchy of their neighborhood groups. MILIT students have the highest self-image, followed by CIVILNEW. While CIVILVET stands somewhere in the middle regarding self-image, Midtown's students exhibit much lower self-perceptions. The lowest self-esteem is of Poortown's students. This hierarchy applies to both school levels.

Having established the hierarchy of academic self-image among the students' groups, we now examine their differences in the perception of school integration. As indicated by the low canonical correlations, integration perceptions are not strongly discriminated by students' neighborhood groups. Recall that the students, on the average, demonstrated a favorable attitude toward the effects of school integration in the investigated domains. However, the discriminant picture revealed is different

**Table 7.4**

**Discriminant Analysis: First Functions of Students' Perceptions by Neighborhood Group within School Level**

| Type of Perception | Elementary and Junior High Schools: Self-Perception | | Integration Perception | | Group Perception | | High School: Self-Perception | | Integration Perception | | Group Perception | |
|---|---|---|---|---|---|---|---|---|---|---|---|---|
| | **S1** | .02 | **I1** | .23 | **G1** | .45 | **S1** | -.28 | **I1** | .65 | **G1** | .48 |
| Discriminating | **S2** | .77 | **I2** | .99 | **G2** | .56 | **S2** | .33 | **I2** | -.41 | **G2** | .53 |
| Variables and | | | | | | | | | | | | |
| Standardized | **S3** | -.06 | **I3** | .05 | **G3** | .35 | **S3** | .39 | **I3** | .06 | **G3** | .54 |
| Discriminant | | | | | | | | | | | | |
| Coefficients | **S4** | .37 | **I4** | -.25 | **G4** | .22 | **S4** | .50 | **I4** | .70 | **G4** | -.04 |
| | **S5** | .03 | | | | | **S5** | .25 | | | | |
| Canonical correlation | | .49 | | .19 | | .41 | | .52 | | .27 | | .25 |
| Wilks' Lambda | | .72 | | .94 | | .81 | | .68 | | .89 | | .89 |
| p ($x^2$ test) | | <.001 | | <.05 | | <.001 | | <.001 | | <.05 | | <.05 |
| **Group Centroids** | | | | | | | | | | | | |
| MILIT | | .63 | | -.24 | | .51 | | .69 | | -.25 | | .05 |
| CIVILNEW | | .48 | | -.10 | | .37 | | .48 | | .06 | | .32 |
| CIVILVET | | .07 | | -.03 | | -.45 | | -.01 | | .81 | | -.43 |
| MIDTOWN | | -.49 | | .21 | | -.29 | | -.43 | | -.35 | | -.28 |
| POORTOWN | | -.66 | | .17 | | -.50 | | -.79 | | .17 | | -.15 |

for each school level. In the elementary and junior high schools, the function rests mainly on the perceived effect of integration on the relationship among classmates. There is a slight tendency of Newtown students (especially MILIT) to perceive this effect as negative, while Oldtown students tend toward a positive view.

Among the high school students the picture is more complex. The function discriminates the groups of students mainly by their attitude toward integration effects on classroom studying and on themselves. To a lesser extent and in an opposite direction, the groups are also discriminated by their perception of the relations among new and veteran students. The group centroids show, however, that the function mainly discriminates CIVILVET from the other student groups, with some smaller differences among the latter. Thus, CIVILVET in high school demonstrates strong support of integration with respect to its effects on themselves and on classroom study, but contends that it has a negative effect on the students' social relations. This ambivalent attitude of CIVILVET students is further exemplified when we move on to the third function.

This function relates to the students' perceptions of differences between the new and the veteran students with respect to academic success, social relationships, socioeconomic status, and the chances of life success. On both school levels, discrimination was obtained mainly by the first three domains. The discriminant power, indicated by the canonical correlations, is stronger at the lower school level, but the discriminant picture of the groups in general is similar for both levels. On both school levels, the students tend to develop rather symmetric group perceptions, in contrast to the asymmetric group perceptions usually found in desegregated school situations. Thus, the new groups (MILIT and CIVILNEW) contend that the new students are better-off than the veterans regarding the three domains, though their tendency for such claims is more noticeable on the lower school levels. The veteran students deny that the new students are superior to them. Such perceptions are especially widespread among Poortown's students in the elementary and junior high schools and among CIVILVET on both school levels.

CIVILVET's perceptions may reflect, in addition to the general trend among the veteran students, their own special position in school. Though they now reside in Newtown, they are still part of the veteran students. Their ambivalence is probably reflected in their denial that the new students are "better" than their veteran counterparts.

Put together, the three functions demonstrate some differences and some similarities between the perceptions of the younger generation and those of the adult Mobiltowners. Like their parents, the students in general hold a positive view of school integration, specifically when asked to state their position on the issue. The clear status hierarchy of their neighborhood groups is well reflected in their self-image. The new students, who are generally of better academic standing than their veteran counterparts, especially those of Poortown, are well aware of this and demonstrate a much higher academic self-esteem. Yet, when it comes to mutual group evaluations, the veteran students demonstrate some resistance to a low group image. All Oldtown students, joined by CIVILVET for their own reasons, insist that they are not inferior to the new students in school. The question examined next relates to the net effect of neighborhood group affiliation on these perceptions.

## THE NET EFFECT OF STUDENTS' NEIGHBORHOOD GROUPS

The differences found among the perceptions of the student groups may, indeed, stem from their neighborhood group affiliation. They may also, however, result from individual differences among the students in status of origin and in academic standing. In order to assess the extent to which group affiliation is the source of the students' perceptions, we reanalyzed the three perception sets within the linear structural relation model.

**Figure 7.1**
**Determinants of Perceptions Among the Elementary and Junior High School Students: A Linear Structural Relation Model**

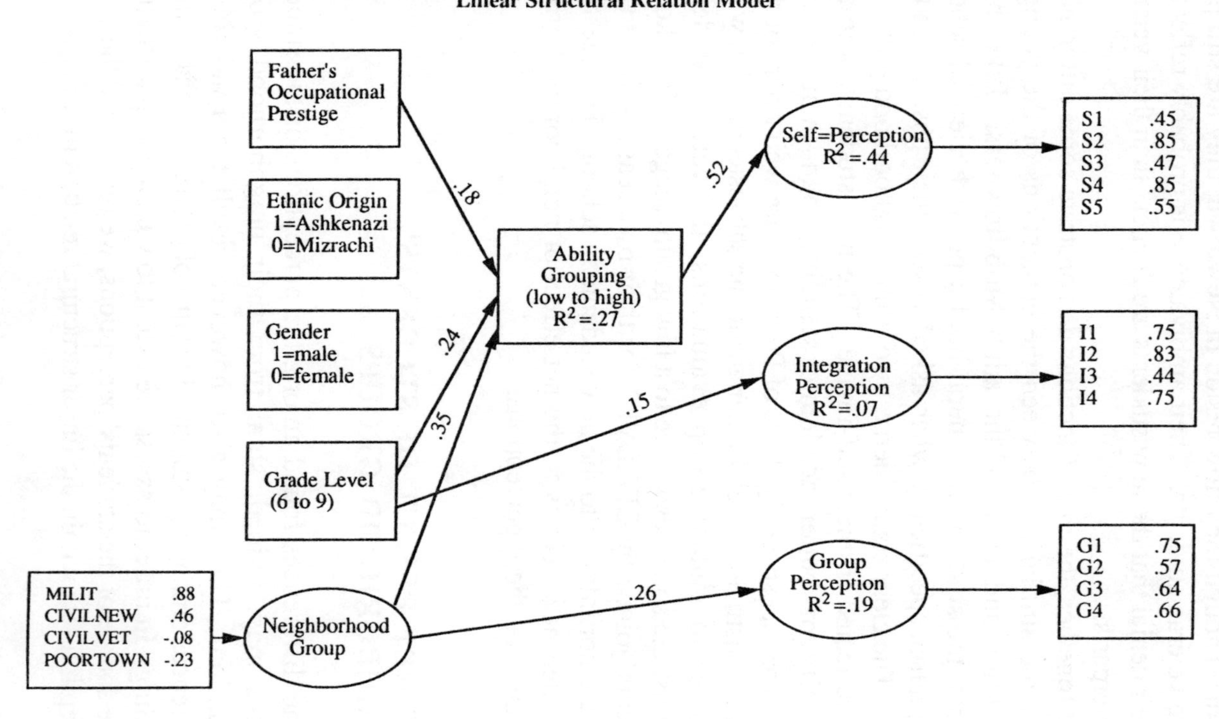


Note: Correlations among the exogenous variables and among the dependent variables, and path coefficients lower than .15 are omitted from the figure.

**Figure 7.2**
**Determinants of Perceptions Among the High School Students: A Linear Sructural Relation Model**

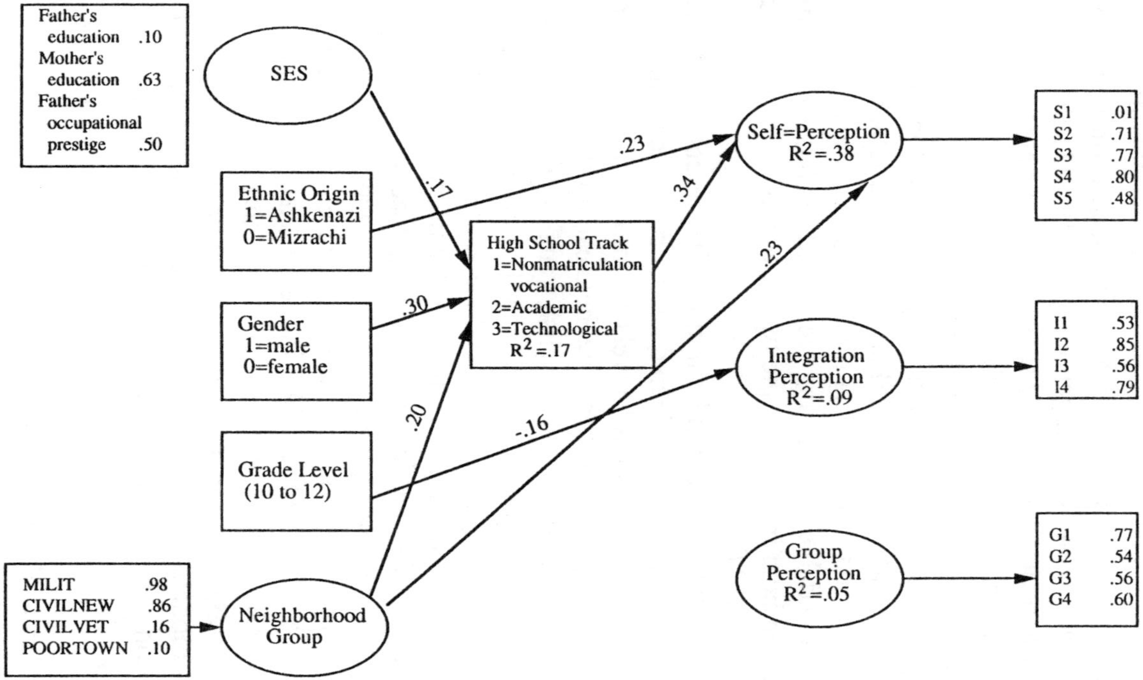

Note: Correlations among the exogenous variables and among the dependent variables, and path coefficients lower than .15 are omitted from the figure.

## The Structure of the Models

Figures 7.1 and 7.2 present the resulting models, one for each school level. The structures of the two models are similar, though they necessarily differ in some specific variables. Both models start with five exogenous variables: (1) the student's status—an inwardly structured socioeconomic status variable for the high school students and father's occupational prestige for the lower-level students (this difference is due to a high proportion of missing data for the other status indicators); (2) ethnic origin; (3) gender; (4) grade level; and (5) an inwardly structured construct of neighborhood groups, using Midtown as a comparison group. The latent variable representing group affiliation is affected most strongly, in both models, by the two new neighborhood groups, especially MILIT.

The mediating variable in both models represents the students' academic standing, as reflected in their division into ability groups at the lower school levels or into high school tracks. Ability grouping was measured by the mean level of the student's grouping in mathematics and English (ranging from 1, the lowest level, to 3, the highest). High school track is a trichotomous variable, measuring the prestige and the academic standard of the student's track. It ranges from the nonmatriculation vocational track, through the matriculation-oriented academic track, to the prestigious technology track, which was established in Mobiltown's high school after the arrival of the new students.

The three dependent variables in the last state of the model are the outwardly structured constructs of the three perception sets. The loadings of the latent perception variables on their indicators in both models present a much more even construction of the perception sets than that obtained in the previous discriminant analysis.

## Analysis of the Models

We start the analysis by examining the determinants of the students' branching in school—their placement in ability groups or in various school tracks. As the two models show, this branching is influenced by both individual-level variables and neighborhood group affiliation. As for individual differences, ability grouping is influenced by grade level and by father's occupational prestige. In the lower grades, a larger proportion of students are placed in lower ability-groups (perhaps because of the larger number of Poortown's students in the elementary school), while those of higher socioeconomic status more often get into higher groupings.

High school tracking is mainly affected by the students' gender and socioeconomic status. In accordance with the gender patterns of tracking in Israeli high schools (Yogev and Ayalon, 1987), girls are placed in the vocational track less often than boys. The finding that socioeconomic status increases the chances of higher tracking, as well as of higher-ability grouping on the lower school levels, is not surprising. It corresponds with the findings of general studies on ability grouping and high school tracking in Israel (e.g., Yogev, 1981; Yogev and Ayalon, 1986).

More significant for our purposes are the independent influences of the neighborhood group construct on the branching of students within school. Neighborhood group affiliation—and, considering the construct indicators, this, for the most part, means belonging to MILIT and CIVILNEW—has a strong independent effect on both ability grouping and high school tracking. Among the elementary and junior high school students, the latent variable representing neighborhood groups has the strongest effect on ability grouping, clearly surpassing the effects of the students' grade level and status of origin.

Among the high school students, the direct influence of neighborhood group on tracking is second only to the gender effect and also surpasses the influence of students' status of origin. Recall that this group effect was obtained after controlling for students' differences in status and in other variables. This means that the new students of MILIT and CIVILNEW are advantaged in terms of school placement on both school levels, beyond the advantage accorded by their parents' status.

Obviously, the major explanation for this may be their higher academic achievements or abilities, which we did not measure. However, the fact remains that the internal school stratification of Mobiltown's students is strongly related to the new neighborhood group structure.

The second stage of both models examines the effects of all the exogenous variables, including neighborhood group, and of the students' school branching on the three perception sets. It appears that the three types of perceptions are directly and indirectly related to different variables.

In the previous discriminant analysis, the students' self-perception was discriminated by the status hierarchy of neighborhood groups. In the present analysis, the neighborhood group variable still has a strong direct effect on the self-image of the high school students. It is, however, joined by an equal effect of ethnic origin and by a stronger, direct effect of tracking. Thus, the high school students tend to develop high self-esteem if they are located in prestigious school tracks, belong to the higher-status neighborhood groups, and are Ashkenazim. This is, by the way, the only case in which we get a direct significant effect of ethnicity on the students' perceptions. As the previous chapters show, ethnicity does not directly influence the perceptions of the adult Mobiltowners either. The self-image of the adolescent Mobiltowners seems to represent a special case in this respect.

The self-perceptions of the students on the lower school levels, are directly influenced only by ability grouping. Neighborhood group affiliation has only an indirect effect on the self-image of these students, through its influence on their ability grouping.

The perception of school integration, endorsed by most students, is very weakly related to their neighborhood groups in the discriminant analysis. Here, too, we find that this perception is weakly explained in general. It is related to one variable only—the students' grade level. The effect of the latter is quite weak, but in an opposite direction for each school level.

In the elementary and junior high schools, the higher the grade level the more positive the attitude toward integration tends to be.

As a matter of standing policy, junior high schools in Israel, more than elementary schools, are required to focus on the integration of various student groups. This may also be the case in Mobiltown. In addition, the integrated elementary schools in town bring together the Newtowners and Poortowners, who represent the extreme status poles. The junior high school is more balanced in its intake of veteran students, and the Newtowners do not constitute the large majority of its student population.

In the high school, however, the effect of grade level is in the opposite direction: students in higher grades tend to endorse school integration less than do those of lower grade levels. It seems that adolescent Mobiltowners tend to develop a more balanced view of their school integration experience, recognizing its disadvantages as well as its benefits.

Turning now to the third set, the mutual group perceptions of new and veteran students, we find that the picture regarding neighborhood group effect is a mixed one. As the high school model shows, group perception is unrelated to any of the other model variables discussed earlier. However, in the elementary and junior high schools, group perception is quite strongly influenced by the students' neighborhood groups, while it remains unrelated to all other variables. The pattern of neighborhood group effect sustains our earlier finding that the students of these schools hold symmetrical group perceptions: both the new and the veteran students believe their group is superior.

In sum, our analysis of the linear structural relation models sustains, to a large extent, the neighborhood group effect on the students' perceptions. It is especially revealed with regard to the self- and group-perceptions of the students on specific school levels. The direct effects of neighborhood group affiliation are quite strong in certain cases, while in others they are mediated by the influence of students' branching in school.

## CONCLUSIONS

We now return to the question posed in the beginning of this chapter. To what extent do the perceptions of the younger generation and their determinants reflect future prospects of coexistence between the new and veteran Mobiltowners?

Similar to their parents, the students endorse the school integration of new and veteran Mobiltowners, at least on the declarative level. When we examine their self-perceptions, however, we get the same neighborhood group hierarchy characterizing their parents' attitudes in various life areas. The higher the status of the neighborhood group, the higher their self-esteem, and vice versa. The direct and mediated effects on the students' self-image sustain the distinctions among various neighborhood groups and carry them over from the adult residents to their offspring. This distinction is particularly noticeable between Poortown's youth, and the children of the new Newtown residents.

Such a perceived hierarchy may carry the seeds of future conflicts. Yet, we also found an encouraging pattern of mutual group perceptions among the students. Contrary to the more common situations of school integration, the new and veteran students of Mobiltown have developed symmetrical group perceptions. This pattern means that both the young Newtowners and the young Poortowners take pride in themselves. Concerning the future, such group perceptions may not lead to an ideal integration according to the melting pot model. However, they may certainly help to create a peaceful coexistence of residential groups, based on the self-confidence of each group, possibly leading to more balanced intergroup relations. On the other hand, the effect of seniority on the group perceptions of the veteran students may fade away with time, as the newcomers, too, become veterans.

Obviously, such future predictions from the students' present attitudes are highly speculative. A better evaluation of the development of intergroup relations in Mobiltown may be reached by returning to the adult inhabitants several years later and examining the changes in their attitudes and lifestyles. This is done in the following chapter.

# 8

# Four Years Later

The previous chapters concentrated on the first stages of the "settle with us" project in Mobiltown. In this chapter we focus on later developments in Mobiltown as they are reflected in a survey conducted four years after the first survey. The various patterns of behavior, attitudes, and perceptions that we described in the first stage may have changed during that period of time; here we focus on the direction of that change.

In general, the effect of time on processes that occur in communities attempting status enhancement through the absorption of higher-status settlers may take either of two opposite directions. It may intensify and stabilize segregative processes, or it may improve intergroup integration. The very fact that the newcomers in a status enhancement project are of a higher SES increases the chances of their formation as distinctive status groups. In time, these status groups may further enforce their interests of exclusion, thus acting as segregative forces in the community. However, it is also possible that the seniority of the veteran residents and their political control of the community will balance these segregative interests by creating positive intergroup contacts, thus leading to a more integrative atmosphere.

Mobiltown's experience in the first stage of the "settle with us" project indicates the prevalence of the segregative forces of a status enhancement project. Not only did the newcomers form distinct status groups, but the veteran political elite also yielded to their particular interests. In the long run, the acquisition of power and influence in the community would probably increase the advantages of the newcomers, thereby enlarging the gaps between them and the veteran residents and further limiting their contacts. Revisiting Mobiltown four years after the initial survey, we would therefore expect the newcomers and veterans to grow further apart. This means less contact in everyday life and further segregated cultural activities, increased segregation of friendship networks, and strengthening of the perception of clear social boundaries among the various neighborhood groups.

However, we should recall that in the first stage, all neighborhood groups expressed satisfaction with the "settle with us" project and with life in Mobiltown in general, despite the segregative tendencies of the newcomers. Obviously, these feelings must have been related to the strong emphasis on an integrative ideology as a banner for the project. Four years later, it should be clearer to all residents that this ideology was somewhat naive. Therefore, it would be illuminating to find out what happened to the perceptions of the various neighborhood groups regarding social integration and satisfaction with life in Mobiltown. These may have become negative, given the processes that occurred. If they nevertheless remain positive, they must be explained on some ground other than the ideology of integration.

## THE FOLLOWUP SURVEY

Since the main purpose of the followup survey was a comparison with the first, the sample and the interview schedule are similar. However, neither the sample nor the interview schedule is completely identical to that of the first stage.

Due to technical difficulties, we were not able to interview the original sample again, which precludes individual-level comparisons. However, since we are interested in the effect of time on behaviors and perceptions of the neighborhood groups, the analyses concentrate on group-level comparisons. The sample of the followup stage is composed of representative subsamples of the seven neighborhood groups. These subsamples are similar to those of the first in terms of socioeconomic characteristics (see Table 8.1), which increases the validity of the comparison.

The interview schedule for the followup stage parallels its predecessor in terms of subjects of inquiry. Most questions are replications of the first stage; some have been rephrased to fit the new situation four years later. A few completely new questions have been added, as they are vital for the analysis of long-term implications of the status enhancement of Mobiltown. We refer to these in the framework of the analysis.

## NEIGHBORHOOD GROUPS AND LIFESTYLE

### Patterns of Consumption

Two aspects of consumption were analyzed in the first stage: degree of consumption and place of consumption. The first aspect is relevant to the issue of the emergence of status groups in Mobiltown. The reexamination of this issue provides a view of the processes occurring in the town. It may reveal that longer contacts between the various groups diminish differences in patterns of consumption, with the less prestigious groups adapting the lifestyle of the higher-status groups. On the other hand, we may find that the higher-status groups, namely the Newtowners, develop a unique lifestyle to emphasize their distinction from the Oldtowners. This would further indicate the crystallization of the Newtowners as a status group.

The second issue is place of consumption. Here either of the following directions is plausible: Mobiltown may become the center of cultural and commercial consumption for the new inhabitants, or the resistance to excessive contacts with the Oldtowners may cause the newcomers either to consume outside

**Table 8.1**
**Characteristics of the New and Veteran Neighborhoods in the Followup Survey**

| | MILIT | CIVILNEW | CIVILVET | MIDNEW | MIDVET | POORNEW | POORVET |
|---|---|---|---|---|---|---|---|
| (a) **Age** (N=556) | | | | | | | |
| Mean | 35.6 | 37.8 | 37.5 | 31.5 | 36.9 | 33.1 | 40.4 |
| SD | 5.9 | 6.6 | 8.0 | 6.7 | 11.0 | 11.3 | 14.4 |
| (b) **Years of Schooling-Men Respondents & Spouses** (N=503) | | | | | | | |
| Mean | 15.1 | 14.1 | 11.7 | 12.6 | 10.7 | 11.0 | 9.8 |
| SD | 2.2 | 2.7 | 3.5 | 2.5 | 3.3 | 2.5 | 2.7 |
| (c) **Years of Schooling-Women Respondents & Spouses** (N=503) | | | | | | | |
| Mean | 13.8 | 13.5 | 11.0 | 12.5 | 10.6 | 10.7 | 9.9 |
| SD | 2.4 | 2.9 | 2.5 | 2.4 | 2.9 | 3.0 | 2.5 |
| (d) **Occupational Prestige-Men Respondents & Spouses** (N=470) | | | | | | | |
| Mean | 80.7 | 73.0 | 57.6 | 62.8 | 50.2 | 51.7 | 43.9 |
| SD | 19.3 | 16.8 | 19.9 | 19.1 | 22.4 | 24.6 | 22.8 |
| (e) **Occupational Prestige-Women Respondents & Spouses** (N=323) | | | | | | | |
| Mean | 60.8 | 63.5 | 26.4 | 45.4 | 24.1 | 25.2 | 15.4 |
| SD | 30.3 | 112.9 | 30.5 | 30.2 | 29.3 | 31.6 | 23.3 |

Table 8.1 (continued)

| | MILIT | CIVILNEW | CIVILVET | MIDNEW | MIDVET | POORNEW | POORVET |
|---|---|---|---|---|---|---|---|
| (f) **Grandfather's Birthplace** (percentages) | | | | | | | |
| Israel | 1.3 | 1.8 | .0 | .0 | 1.1 | .0 | .0 |
| Asia-Africa | 23.4 | 45.0 | 91.4 | 63.0 | 82.6 | 66.7 | 91.9 |
| Europe-America | 75.3 | 53.2 | 8.6 | 37.0 | 16.3 | 33.3 | 8.1 |
| Total (N=562) | 100.0 | 100.0 | 100.0 | 100.0 | 100.0 | 100.0 | 100.0 |
| (g) **Respondent's Birthplace** (percentages) | | | | | | | |
| Israel | 64.9 | 57.1 | 28.6 | 72.6 | 39.4 | 61.5 | 29.4 |
| Asia-Africa | 11.7 | 27.7 | 65.7 | 13.7 | 45.7 | 28.2 | 64.7 |
| Europe-America | 23.4 | 15.2 | 5.7 | 13.7 | 14.9 | 10.3 | 5.9 |
| Total (N=566) | 100.0 | 100.0 | 100.0 | 100.0 | 100.0 | 100.0 | 100.0 |

Mobiltown or to develop alternative commercial and cultural centers for their own use.

We begin the comparison with the issue of cultural consumption (Table 8.2). The most prominent finding in this domain is the growing tendency of MILIT to participate in cultural activities inside Mobiltown (see Table 4.1 for the first stage). This is particularly noticeable in comparison to the other neighborhood groups, where we found either slight changes (in both directions) or stability.

Participation in clubs for children reveals an interesting pattern. There is a consistent tendency of increased participation among the children of the new residents, regardless of neighborhood. Here again, the most prominent increase pertains to MILIT (about 93 percent of their children participate in such activities in the second period). Concomitant to the growing participation of young newcomers in these clubs is an apparent decrease in the respective proportion of veterans. It appears that these clubs, which used to belong mainly to the veteran residents, are undergoing a significant change in composition. They have become clubs of the newcomers, especially MILIT. Participation in clubs for children takes place almost exclusively in Mobiltown. However, they do not seem to be very effective in enhancing the contact between veterans and newcomers.

In the first stage, the neighborhood groups were differentiated only with respect to a few of the many areas of consumption investigated: car repair services, the library, and summer camps. Are there any changes four years later? Apparently, there are. MILIT and CIVILNEW are still characterized by a high tendency to use car repair services. However, there is an increase in the proportion of users of this service in all neighborhood groups, which may indicate some change in lifestyle under the influence of the Newtowners. The differentiation between the neighborhood groups in this respect is reduced.

Concomitant to the increase in the proportion of car owners, there appears to be a decrease in the tendency to use Mobiltown's related services. However, the pattern that pertains to car repair services is unique. In many other domains, Mobiltown emerges

**Table 8.2**
**Patterns of Consumption of the Neighborhood Groups in the Followup Survey**

| | | MILIT | CIVILNEW | CIVILVET | MIDNEW | MIDVET | POORNEW | POORVET |
|---|---|---|---|---|---|---|---|---|
| **Cultural Activities** | A | 92.2 | 79.5 | 65.7 | 51.4 | 44.7 | 33.3 | 29.4 |
| (N=565) | B | 52.1 | 67.4 | 47.8 | 37.8 | 28.6 | 30.8 | 37.5 |
| **Clubs for Adults** | A | 27.6 | 26.8 | 25.7 | 26.4 | 24.7 | 10.3 | 11.9 |
| (N=562) | B | 90.5 | 80.0 | 77.8 | 94.7 | 91.3 | 75.0 | 43.8 |
| **Clubs for Children** | A | 93.1 | 78.1 | 79.4 | 46.8 | 55.4 | 35.1 | 41.7 |
| (N=513) | B | 100.0 | 100.0 | 96.3 | 100.0 | 97.8 | 100.0 | 98.0 |
| **Bank Services*** (N=565) | B | 8.7 | 22.0 | 100.0 | 65.8 | 92.6 | 81.1 | 94.7 |
| **Car Repair Services** | A | 94.8 | 90.9 | 82.9 | 69.9 | 63.8 | 61.5 | 53.0 |
| (N=562) | B | 42.5 | 46.0 | 41.3 | 35.3 | 61.9 | 39.3 | 44.1 |
| **Hairdresser** * (N=563) | B | 78.9 | 79.0 | 87.5 | 64.7 | 87.4 | 74.3 | 86.9 |
| **Summer Camps** | A | 85.7 | 79.2 | 94.3 | 48.6 | 60.2 | 51.3 | 50.7 |
| (N=556) | B | 84.8 | 71.4 | 87.9 | 77.1 | 89.3 | 70.0 | 83.8 |
| **Library** | A | 93.5 | 88.1 | 88.2 | 67.1 | 64.9 | 53.8 | 57.8 |
| (N=561) | B | 84.7 | 79.2 | 96.7 | 73.5 | 88.5 | 71.4 | 84.9 |
| **Swimming Pool** | A | 100.0 | 97.3 | 94.1 | 87.7 | 87.2 | 84.6 | 74.3 |
| (N=565) | B | 96.1 | 90.8 | 100.0 | 78.1 | 89.0 | 84.8 | 87.1 |
| **Videotape Library** | A | 41.6 | 55.0 | 57.1 | 27.4 | 45.1 | 35.9 | 33.6 |
| (N=558) | B | 53.1 | 60.0 | 75.0 | 45.0 | 53.7 | 57.1 | 62.2 |
| **Purchase for Children** | A | 98.7 | 89.9 | 97.1 | 87.5 | 87.0 | 89.7 | 71.1 |
| (N=559) | B | 84.2 | 74.5 | 67.6 | 47.6 | 67.5 | 60.0 | 76.0 |

**Table 8.2 (continued)**

| | | MILIT | CIVILNEW | CIVILVET | MIDNEW | MIDVET | POORNEW | POORVET |
|---|---|---|---|---|---|---|---|---|
| **Purchase of Books, Records** (N=559) | A | 97.4 | 89.9 | 97.1 | 79.5 | 81.5 | 71.8 | 69.4 |
| | B | 80.0 | 60.2 | 67.6 | 41.4 | 57.3 | 42.9 | 59.1 |
| **Groceries*** (N=566) | B | 94.8 | 97.3 | 100.0 | 98.6 | 100.0 | 94.7 | 99.3 |
| **Purchase of Household Products** (N=562) | B | 76.6 | 80.2 | 85.3 | 81.4 | 91.4 | 87.2 | 91.2 |
| **Purchase of Clothes and Shoes*** (N=563) | B | 28.6 | 33.3 | 47.1 | 24.3 | 57.0 | 56.8 | 62.4 |
| **Periodic Shopping*** (N=560) | B | 6.8 | 9.6 | 18.2 | 8.3 | 17.9 | 35.3 | 35.8 |
| **Percent Using:** | | | | | | | | |
| The market (N=537) | | 78.1 | 72.5 | 88.6 | 85.9 | 91.5 | 89.5 | 97.1 |
| Old Commercial Center (N=490) | | 51.4 | 50.0 | 41.4 | 58.5 | 69.5 | 52.6 | 63.1 |
| New Commercial Center (N=511) | | 96.0 | 95.0 | 77.4 | 50.8 | 49.4 | 60.5 | 55.9 |
| **Country Club** (N=560) | | | | | | | | |
| Members | | 72.7 | 64.9 | 54.3 | 13.7 | 9.7 | 5.4 | 6.7 |
| Don't visit | | 7.8 | 12.6 | 2.9 | 49.3 | 43.0 | 67.6 | 59.7 |

Note: For each activity or item, A is the percent of neighborhood group's respondents who participate or consume the item in general; B is the percent of respondents who participate or consume the item in Mobiltown, out of the total participants or consumers.

* A is omitted since consumption is general.

as a commercial center for its new inhabitants. The change is particularly prominent among MILIT and to a certain degree among CIVILNEW. These two groups, who initially preferred services outside Mobiltown, exhibit a striking change. Four years later, they prefer Mobiltown's hairdressers, swimming pool, videotape library, and bookstores.

The earlier impression that Mobiltown is not emerging as a "bedroom town" for its inhabitants is now strengthened. The newcomers exhibit a clear tendency to consume inside the town. What are the implications of this phenomenon in terms of integration of the various groups? Several items that were not included in the earlier interview provide some information on this issue. These items deal with the utilization of the open market, the old commercial center, and two newly established centers in Newtown—the new commercial center and the water park. It appears that the differentiation among the neighborhood groups in terms of utilization of the market and the old center is marginal. The existence of the new commercial center does not stop Newtowners from using the commercial facilities in Oldtown. Similarly, Oldtowners do visit Newtown's new center (although less than Newtowners, especially the new inhabitants). Each group reveals some tendency to prefer its own commercial center, but the pattern revealed in the followup stage leaves much room for intergroup contact.

The tendency of the Newtowners to emerge as status groups with unique lifestyles differentiating them from Oldtowners is revealed in the patterns of utilization of the water park. The differences between Newtowners and Oldtowners in terms of membership in the water park are striking. Apparently, it is Newtown's water park. Actually, the foundation of the park was initiated by the Newtowners, who did not conceal their wish to minimize Oldtown's participation. The high subscription rate and ticket prices probably play a central role in preventing Oldtowners from either membership or even casual visits to the park.

The four-year period did not produce any notable change in Mobiltowners' satisfaction with the services. Most changes are

**Table 8.3**
**Satisfaction with Services by Neighborhood Group in the Followup Survey**

**Percent Satisfied and Very Satisfied**

| | Education | Culture | Welfare | Sanitation | Health | Religious | General Satisfaction |
|---|---|---|---|---|---|---|---|
| **Newtown** | | | | | | | |
| MILIT | 88.3 | 67.6 | 72.7 | 60.5 | 75.7 | 90.0 | 94.8 |
| CIVILNEW | 87.5 | 65.6 | 71.1 | 61.7 | 69.7 | 82.6 | 90.8 |
| CIVILVET | 76.4 | 64.5 | 62.1 | 65.8 | 74.3 | 75.0 | 88.6 |
| **Oldtown** | | | | | | | |
| MIDNEW | 96.0 | 64.7 | 61.1 | 54.5 | 68.1 | 83.9 | 76.5 |
| MIDVET | 71.4 | 61.0 | 71.8 | 59.3 | 70.0 | 76.8 | 78.3 |
| POORNEW | 67.9 | 40.7 | 62.9 | 40.0 | 61.1 | 80.0 | 68.6 |
| POORVET | 78.5 | 54.7 | 55.9 | 43.8 | 77.5 | 87.9 | 78.2 |
| TOTAL | 82.2 | 61.0 | 63.5 | 54.7 | 72.0 | 82.7 | 82.9 |
| N | 564 | 564 | 556 | 564 | 562 | 557 | 562 |

minor, and their direction is positive. As Table 8.3 shows, four years later the Mobiltowners are even more satisfied with the services and with life in the town in general. An apparent change in attitude is revealed in one domain only—cultural activities. Four years later, Mobiltowners exhibit much higher satisfaction with the cultural services. This is especially prominent among MILIT and POORVET, the least satisfied groups in the first stage. This indicates a general enhancement in Mobiltown's cultural services, not an improvement aimed at the needs of any particular group.

### Friendship Networks

As Table 8.4 shows, the four-year period did not produce notable changes in the pattern of the friendship networks of the Mobiltowners. Parallel to the first stage, the majority of the respondents report that they have friends in Mobiltown. This is particularly noticeable among the Newtowners. Some changes do exist in the area of intraneighborhood friendship contacts. Among most neighborhood groups, there appears to be some decline in the proportion of such relationships. Although the changes are marginal in magnitude, they may indicate some degree of desegregation within the neighborhood groups.

The pattern revealed among CIVILVET is exceptional in this respect. In comparison with the first stage, they have almost doubled their intraneighborhood contacts. As they were the only group to move from Oldtown to Newtown, it was not surprising in the first stage to find that most friends of CIVILVET were Oldtowners. Four years later, the members of this group have established new contacts in their new neighborhood.

On the whole, the pattern revealed in the first stage is replicated, with the new Newtowners exhibiting the highest degree of intraneighborhood relationships. As noted, social contacts among members of the neighborhood may serve as a resource in the struggle for social power and influence in the community. This trend is strengthened four years later, since

**Table 8.4**

**Distribution of Friendship Networks by Neighborhood Group in the Followup Survey**

| | Have Friends in Mobiltown | Have Friends in Same Neighborhood | Most Friends New in Mobiltown |
|---|---|---|---|
| **Newtown** | | | |
| MILIT | 90.8 | 87.2 | 85.5 |
| CIVILNEW | 94.6 | 72.6 | 62.9 |
| CIVILVET | 100.0 | 54.5 | 11.8 |
| **Oldtown** | | | |
| MIDNEW | 80.6 | 59.3 | 48.3 |
| MIDVET | 87.2 | 45.1 | 7.3 |
| POORNEW | 76.9 | 48.4 | 32.3 |
| POORVET | 4.6 | 46.1 | 12.0 |
| Total | 88.8 | 60.0 | 38.4 |
| N | 565 | 502 | 503 |

CIVILVET, who might have been considered "outsiders" in Newtown, adapt to their new social milieu. Because they are part of Oldtown's elite, the adaptation of CIVILVET may contribute substantially to Newtown's acquisition of social power. However, the members of CIVILVET also report many social relations with Oldtowners, which means that at present they can be considered as a "bridge" between the two parts of Mobiltown.

## MUTUAL PERCEPTIONS

### Perceptions of Groups

The four-year period did not cause Mobiltowners to change their view that the community is divided into various groups.

However, Table 8.5 shows a sharp decline in the proportion of Poortowners who share this perception. In general, Newtowners and MIDNEW exhibit a higher tendency to perceive social divisions in Mobiltown. As we keep in mind that many POORNEW are Mobiltowners who left their town temporarily, it appears that the newcomers are those who emphasize the distinction between the various groups.

Analysis of the sources of distinction differentiates the newcomers in Newtowners from the other neighborhood groups. MILIT and CIVILNEW tend to perceive dichotomous distinctions (about 50 percent of each mentioned either the Newtown-Oldtown or the veterans-newcomers distinction). On the other hand, Poortowners and MIDVET tend to describe Mobiltown as divided between various neighborhoods; that is, their perception is less dichotomized.

A comparison with the first stage indicates an obvious decline in the dichotomous perceptions among all groups. This impression is strengthened by the reactions of the respondents to two items that are directly concerned with inner differentiations in Newtown and in Oldtown. Almost all the neighborhood groups, Newtowners and Oldtowners, are much more conscious, four years later, of internal differentiations in Newtown. CIVILVET is the only exception. Since it constitutes a unique group in Newtown, it is no surprise to find that CIVILVET was conscious of that inner differentiation at the early stages of the settlement of Newtown. A similar change has occurred in the perceptions of the inner differentiations in Oldtown. All seven groups are now more sensitive to the variation among Oldtowners. However, Newtown is perceived as more differentiated than Oldtown by all neighborhood groups. This has not changed during the four-year period. An additional pattern that remains stable is the apparent sensitivity of the Newtowners to inner differentiations both in their own neighborhood and in Oldtown.

It is interesting to note that the new Newtowners, who mention the dichotomous divisions, are more sensitive to in-neighborhood differentiations, while the Oldtowners, who

**Table 8.5**
**Perceptions of Groups in Mobiltown in the Followup Survey**

| | MILIT | CIVILNEW | CIVILVET | MIDNEW | MIDVET | POORNEW | POORVET |
|---|---|---|---|---|---|---|---|
| (a) Percentage agreeing: Mobiltown is divided into different groups (N=556) | 76.6 | 63.9 | 54.3 | 69.9 | 46.2 | 39.5 | 31.1 |
| **Mobiltown is divided into:** | | | | | | | |
| Newtown/Oldtown | 24.1 | 23.1 | 7.4 | 15.6 | 11.8 | 7.7 | 18.8 |
| Newcomers/veterans | 20.4 | 2.6 | 21.4 | 17.8 | 11.8 | 15.4 | 9.4 |
| Various neighborhoods | 7.4 | 6.2 | 7.1 | 22.2 | 35.3 | 38.5 | 43.8 |
| Different groups exist in Newtown | 61.4 | 73.6 | 70.6 | 49.3 | 54.4 | 40.0 | 48.7 |
| Different groups exist in Oldtown | 56.3 | 57.4 | 51.5 | 39.7 | 40.7 | 20.0 | 32.3 |
| (b) Percentage agreeing: The following group obtains its proper share: | | | | | | | |
| MILIT (N=533) | 90.5 | 97.1 | 96.9 | 98.5 | 100.0 | 100.0 | 96.9 |
| CIVILNEW (N=518) | 90.9 | 86.3 | 83.9 | 95.5 | 98.9 | 94.6 | 97.6 |
| CIVILVET (N=504) | 88.5 | 77.9 | 75.0 | 90.8 | 96.7 | 89.2 | 93.5 |
| POORTOWN (N=493) | 70.2 | 41.4 | 56.7 | 45.3 | 40.7 | 16.2 | 21.3 |
| MIDVET (N=477) | 72.7 | 47.6 | 43.3 | 42.9 | 31.8 | 19.4 | 19.5 |
| MIDNEW (N=466) | 75.5 | 52.5 | 48.3 | 48.3 | 44.2 | 28.6 | 28.5 |

**Table 8.5 (continued)**

| | MILIT | CIVILNEW | CIVILVET | MIDNEW | MIDVET | POORNEW | POORVET |
|---|---|---|---|---|---|---|---|
| (c) The services of the local council mostly benefit (N=558): | | | | | | | |
| MILIT | 18.4 | 34.9 | 52.9 | 30.6 | 49.5 | 56.4 | 40.7 |
| CIVILNEW | 1.3 | 11.0 | 2.9 | 11.1 | 17.2 | 12.8 | 21.5 |
| CIVILVET | .0 | 1.8 | 2.9 | .0 | .0 | 2.6 | 3.0 |
| POORTOWN | 22.4 | 16.5 | 20.6 | 2.8 | .0 | .0 | 3.7 |
| MIDVET | 7.9 | 2.8 | .0 | .0 | .0 | 5.1 | .7 |
| MIDNEW | .0 | .0 | .0 | .0 | .0 | 2.6 | .7 |
| No particular group | 27.3 | 13.8 | 11.8 | 30.6 | 11.8 | 5.1 | 7.4 |
| (d) Percent agreeing: The education system equally benefits all groups (N=532) | 83.1 | 82.2 | 85.3 | 87.5 | 89.0 | 88.2 | 84.8 |

describe the divisions less definitively, express a "whole group" image. This may indicate that perceptions of sources of divisions and of inner differentiation are not necessarily complementary. Apparently, the perception of the new Newtowners that each neighborhood is composed of different groups does not prevent them from seeing the centrality of the Newtown-Oldtown conflict, which blurs all other divisions. However, the overall decline in dichotomous perceptions during the four-year period might indicate some move away from the emphasis of the Newtown-Oldtown differentiation, perhaps to more subtle sources of division.

## Images of Power

In the first stage of the study, we found that Newtowners were perceived as the main possessors of social power by themselves and especially by the Oldtowners. What has happened to these images during the elapsed period? The items that pertain to this issue (part b of Table 8.5) deal mainly with images of the distribution of resources in the community. The reactions of the respondents to a general question on this subject reveal almost total consensus among the neighborhood groups that the Newtowners have received their fair share in the distribution of resources. On average, Oldtowners express a higher evaluation of the Newtowners' power than do the latter themselves. This pattern has not changed since the previous survey.

A notable weakening of the consensus appears with regard to the power of the Oldtowners. The Poortowners, both veterans and newcomers, express blatant feelings of relative deprivation. According to them, Oldtowners as a whole and especially their own neighborhood have been deprived. Midtowners share this view; more than 50 percent perceive themselves as deprived. However, higher proportions share the Poortowners' view of the deprivation of their neighborhood. Newtowners are divided with respect to the deprivation of Oldtown. Both CIVILVET and CIVILNEW do not believe that Oldtown gets its proper share of resources, while a high proportion of MILIT (more than 70 percent) state that Oldtown does get its due share. The unique attitude of MILIT in this respect may stem from its reservations regarding the provision of welfare and financial aid to Oldtowners. MILIT do not seem to disagree with the general consensus on the advantages of Newtown, but they tend to ascribe it to their own actions. Their attitude toward Oldtown's power may reflect their view that those who do more get more.

When the general issue of distribution of resources is divided into particular areas (part c of Table 8.5), the picture is less straightforward. When asked which groups benefit from the local council services, about one-third of the respondents report either that they do not know or that there is no such group. However, the general tendency (about 40 to 50 percent of the various groups) is to view MILIT as the main beneficiary of these services. MILIT does not seem to agree with this view. The four-year period has only strengthened their reluctance to admit the existence of any privileges whatsoever. When asked about the least beneficiary group in terms of the services of the local council, a large minority of the Oldtowners mention Poortown. As expected, Newtowners, and especially MILIT, do not seem to share this view.

Several items show a complete absence of feelings of relative deprivation in the realm of education. As we have already seen, the Mobiltowners are very satisfied with their education system. Here we also find that about 85 percent of the respondents, with minor intergroup differences, reject the notion that the education system in Mobiltown operates in favor of any particular neighborhood group.

The general picture, however, indicates the common feeling among Mobiltowners that the Newtowners are the main possessors of social power. This common feeling appears to be amorphous; when respondents are asked to evaluate Newtowners' advantage in specific areas, the answers become less definite.

## Attitude toward Social Integration

We have seen that a short while after the initial settlement of Newtown, the common Mobiltowners' attitude toward the integration of newcomers and veteran residents was quite positive. This general pattern has not changed during the four-year period.

Similar to the previous findings, Table 8.6 shows that integration is perceived as particularly beneficial in the education system. It is also perceived quite positively in areas of municipal technical services and community activity. In these areas, the attitude of the stronger groups, namely the Newtowners, tends to be more favorable than that of the weaker ones.

This positive picture of the overall situation is altered significantly when we examine the contribution of social integration to political life. Most Mobiltowners reject the notion that integration is beneficial to the political situation. This unique attitude toward the effect of integration in this realm was also prominent in the first survey; apparently, it has been sustained during the elapsed period. It probably stems from the Mobiltowners' understanding that a struggle for political control is inevitable. The Newtowners and the Oldtowners are quite divided politically, with the former striving for control and the latter defending their existing privileges.

When the reference to social integration is more abstract (part b of Table 8.6), the attitude is very favorable. More than 70 percent of the various neighborhood groups believe in complete integration. The only group that reveals reservations is MILIT, although here, too, the majority supports complete integration. To summarize, it appears that the four-year period has only intensified Mobiltowners' perceptions of the benefits of social integration. It is interesting that the strongest social group, MILIT, which perceives integration as beneficial in several concrete areas, is the least supportive of this concept on the abstract level. With most other groups, particularly the Oldtowners, the picture is reversed. They are aware of their relative disadvantage under social integration, but they support it

**Table 8.6**
**Attitudes Toward Social Integration in the Followup Survey**

| | MILIT | CIVILNEW | CIVILVET | MIDNEW | MIDVET | POORNEW | POORVET |
|---|---|---|---|---|---|---|---|
| (a) Percent agreeing: Integration is beneficial for: | | | | | | | |
| Education (N=564) | 68.9 | 58.5 | 62.9 | 50.7 | 72.3 | 69.3 | 52.6 |
| Municipal technical services (N=556) | 62.4 | 51.8 | 60.0 | 46.5 | 51.6 | 45.9 | 39.7 |
| Community activities (N=550) | 76.7 | 62.8 | 67.7 | 44.4 | 58.6 | 40.5 | 43.0 |
| Political life (N=535) | 22.4 | 32.4 | 35.3 | 17.4 | 38.2 | 26.3 | 18.5 |
| (b) Should the neighborhoods integrate? (N=563): | | | | | | | |
| Complete integration | 62.3 | 72.1 | 80.0 | 75.0 | 89.4 | 79.5 | 74.1 |
| Partial integration | 27.3 | 19.8 | 14.3 | 20.8 | 6.4 | 10.3 | 6.7 |
| No integration | 6.5 | 3.6 | 2.9 | 4.2 | 2.1 | 5.1 | 8.1 |
| (c) Attitudes toward school integration (N=560): | | | | | | | |
| Too much integration | 25.0 | 15.5 | 14.3 | 20.8 | 25.8 | 35.9 | 25.2 |
| Enough | 56.6 | 50.9 | 40.0 | 29.0 | 10.3 | 10.3 | 20.7 |
| Insufficient | 14.5 | 25.5 | 40.0 | 18.1 | 17.2 | 25.6 | 22.2 |
| Don't know | 3.9 | 8.2 | 5.7 | 31.9 | 28.0 | 28.2 | 31.9 |

when it is presented more abstractly. This may indicate MILIT's segregative tendencies, which are strong in spite of its tangible advantages in the integrative situation. The attitudes that pertain to political life might indicate future processes: when intergroup conflict is clear and obvious, the notion of social integration is rejected.

## THE POLITICAL DIMENSION

The findings of the followup survey differ most from those of the previous one regarding political life. This produces the impression that prominent changes have occurred in the political scene in Mobiltown. However, a visitor would have a hard time finding these changes. The ruling elite is still composed of veterans, and the mayor is still B., who was nominated by M. as his successor. In the recent local elections, B. was elected by a majority of the residents as Mobiltown's mayor. His party, the LIKUD, still dominates the municipality. Does this imply that Mobiltown's political life is stable? The perceptions of the Mobiltowners indicate otherwise, as indicated by Table 8.7.

Part a of the table reveals that only a negligible minority views CIVILVET, or any other veteran group, as dominant, in contrast to the earlier results, which indicated a tendency to view the veterans as the strongest group politically. The newcomers, especially MILIT, are viewed as the most influential group in town. MILIT itself is still reluctant to admit its possession of power. CIVILVET's apparent tendency to identify MILIT as the powerful group probably reflects their awareness of the decline in their power, despite their ruling position.

The vagueness of the political perceptions held by the Mobiltowners is indicated by the high proportion who admit that they actually do not know which group is ruling the city. This uncertainty also prevails with regard to identifying the least influential group (part b). Although a substantial minority in all neighborhood groups assign the Poortowners to that category, a

**Table 8.7**
**Perceptions of Political Power in the Followup Survey**

| | MILIT | CIVILNEW | CIVILVET | MIDNEW | MIDVET | POORNEW | POORVET |
|---|---|---|---|---|---|---|---|
| (a) Most influential group today (N=556) | | | | | | | |
| MILIT | 24.0 | 40.2 | 57.1 | 27.8 | 34.4 | 30.8 | 26.7 |
| CIVILNEW | 4.0 | 13.1 | 8.6 | 5.6 | 14.0 | 12.8 | 11.9 |
| CIVILVET | 2.7 | 1.9 | 2.9 | 1.4 | 3.2 | 5.1 | 2.2 |
| POORTOWNERS | 4.0 | 2.8 | 2.9 | .0 | 3.2 | .0 | 2.2 |
| MIDVET | 16.0 | 8.4 | .0 | 2.8 | 6.5 | 7.7 | 8.1 |
| MIDNEW | .0 | .0 | .0 | .0 | 1.1 | 2.6 | 1.5 |
| No Group | 9.3 | 5.6 | 11.4 | 12.5 | 3.2 | 2.6 | 8.1 |
| Don't Know | 40.0 | 28.0 | 17.1 | 50.0 | 34.4 | 38.5 | 39.3 |
| (b) Least influential group (N=555) | | | | | | | |
| MILIT | 10.0 | 5.7 | 8.6 | 2.8 | 5.3 | 7.7 | 4.4 |
| CIVILNEW | 4.0 | 13.3 | 2.9 | .0 | 2.1 | 7.7 | 3.7 |
| CIVILVET | 2.7 | 1.9 | 5.7 | .0 | 3.2 | .0 | 4.4 |
| POORTOWNERS | 21.3 | 21.9 | 34.3 | 20.8 | 31.9 | 35.9 | 23.7 |
| MIDVET | 6.7 | 4.8 | 17.1 | 8.3 | 11.7 | 2.6 | 15.6 |
| MIDNEW | 2.7 | 10.5 | .0 | .0 | 1.1 | 2.6 | .7 |
| No group | 6.7 | 5.7 | 11.4 | 12.5 | 5.3 | 2.6 | 9.6 |
| Don't know | 45.3 | 36.2 | 20.0 | 55.6 | 39.4 | 41.0 | 37.8 |

**Table 8.7 (continued)**

| | MILIT | CIVILNEW | CIVILVET | MIDNEW | MIDVET | POORNEW | POORVET |
|---|---|---|---|---|---|---|---|
| (c) Most influential group in five years (N=549) | | | | | | | |
| MILIT | 60.8 | 48.6 | 65.7 | 41.2 | 63.7 | 57.9 | 56.0 |
| CIVILNEW | 17.6 | 33.0 | 20.0 | 29.4 | 18.7 | 23.7 | 20.1 |
| CIVILVET | .0 | 4.6 | 2.9 | 5.9 | 3.3 | 5.3 | 3.7 |
| POORTOWNERS | 2.7 | .0 | .0 | 1.5 | .0 | 1.5 | 23.7 |
| MIDVET | 8.1 | 5.5 | 8.6 | 1.5 | 5.5 | .0 | 3.7 |
| MIDNEW | 1.4 | .0 | .0 | 2.9 | .0 | .0 | .0 |
| (d) Most influential people in five years (N= 521) | | | | | | | |
| Mainly veterans | 13.7 | 9.5 | 2.9 | 4.6 | 6.9 | 11.1 | 10.7 |
| Mainly newcomers | 54.8 | 60.0 | 61.8 | 47.7 | 56.3 | 44.4 | 41.3 |
| Both | 31.7 | 30.5 | 35.3 | 47.7 | 36.8 | 44.4 | 47.9 |

higher proportion of all respondents (except CIVILVET) do not identify any particular group as the least influential.

The vagueness of the political images completely disappears when the Mobiltowners are asked about power relations in the near future—five years later (part c). The anticipation of the future dominance of the newcomers in Newtown, especially MILIT, is straightforward. In contrast to its reactions regarding the present, MILIT perceives itself as dominating Mobiltown in the near future and does not hesitate to admit it. CIVILNEW perceives MILIT as the future ruling group, but ascribes substantial future influence to itself as well.

The perceptions of the increasing power of the newcomers are revealed again in part d of the table. The tendency to identify the newcomers as the future holders of social power has strengthened during the four-year period. The Newtowners perceive the newcomers as those who will possess the most social power in the future, while the Oldtowners reveal more integrative perceptions. It is interesting that CIVILVET is the most pessimistic regarding the future power of the Oldtowners; this is evidently an additional indication of their sensitivity to the decreased power.

Apparently, the four-year period has established the perception of the decreasing power of the veterans among all neighborhood groups. This probably stems from a combination of processes—the increasing dominance of the newcomers, especially MILIT, in school committees, the success of the Newtowners in imposing their demands on the city council, and other such developments. The most prominent success of the Newtowners, at least on the symbolic level, is perhaps the nomination of a CIVILNEW member as the Labor party's candidate for mayor. Although his success in the local elections was modest, the capacity of the Newtowners to put their man at the head of a major political party probably contributes to a general feeling that the distribution of power in Mobiltown is in a process of significant change. Apparently, the newcomers are taking control of Mobiltown's foci of power gradually. The Mobiltowners are so aware of this process that the dominance of the veteran elite in the municipality does not prevent them from perceiving the Newtowners as the present — and more so, the future — rulers of the city. This may imply that the Mobiltowners view the present dominance of the Oldtowners in the municipality as temporary.

## CONCLUSIONS: TOWARD INTEGRATION OR SEGREGATION?

The followup survey in Mobiltown does not reveal new trends and dramatic changes in the organization of social life. However, several conclusions that seemed tentative in the first stage are substantially supported.

The findings generally indicate an increase in the segregative tendencies of the new Newtowners. The clearest segregative tendencies, as well as processes of crystallization as a status group, are revealed among MILIT. This group is quite strongly differentiated from its neighbors in Newtown in behavior and, to a large degree, in perceptions. MILIT supplies the highest proportion of participants in the most segregative activities, such as clubs for children and the water park. Segregative tendencies are also exhibited by the high proportion of intraneighborhood friendships and the low rates of intergroup associations. MILIT demonstrates unique perceptions of the allocation of the resources of Mobiltown. It is the only group that disagrees with the common consensus on the deprivation of Poortown. Being aware of the disadvantage of the Poortowners, MILIT's reaction to the issue of their deprivation might even be interpreted as hostile.

MILIT is an extreme example of the segregative tendencies prevailing in Mobiltown. It is clear that these tendencies become stronger than those of social integration as time passes. Yet, we cannot ignore some indications of increased cooperation or similarity among the neighborhood groups. The four years have narrowed the distance between Newtown and Oldtown in several aspects of lifestyle. The distinction between the various groups in terms of commercial consumption has been marginal from the very beginning. The main change in this area is the emergence of Mobiltown as a commercial center for all its inhabitants. Both Newtowners and Oldtowners use the same commercial centers. The new center, which is located in Newtown, is also used by Oldtowners. Apparently, the commercial centers do create contacts between the various neighborhood groups. However, the high rates of intraneighborhood friendships indicate that intergroup contacts remain specific and superficial. The intergroup contacts, although limited in nature, cause a general increase in the sensitivity to the inner differentiation in both Oldtown and Newtown. However, this does not appear to change the common view that the main sources of social conflict are either the Newtown-Oldtown dichotomy or the distinction between newcomers and veteran residents. This indicates that time has not changed the perceptions of the social divisions in Mobiltown.

In fact, the recognition of these social divisions has even increased, in the sense that all Mobiltowners now agree that MILIT and CIVILNEW will rule Mobiltown in the near future. In the first survey, all groups showed a higher tendency to depict the newcomers and veterans as the joint future rulers of the community.

Despite this realization of the superior power of the Newtowners, our findings indicate that satisfaction with life in town has increased for all Mobiltowners, and that the attitudes toward social integration have also become more positive in general. Indeed, most Mobiltowners agree that social integration has not been beneficial for the political life of the community. Nevertheless, they hold a positive attitude toward the "complete integration" of all neighborhoods. This general attitude may be explained away by social desirability, but it seems to us that it may very well reflect the satisfaction of all residents with the benefits that the "settle with us" project has brought to Mobiltown as a community. In particular, all groups are satisfied with the positive effects that "integration" (namely the newcomers) has had in the spheres of education, municipal services, and community activities. The only group showing less satisfaction with changes in these areas is POORVET, consisting of the truly disadvantaged. For most Mobiltowners, however, integration means an improvement in life quality: the newcomers have succeeded in establishing the lifestyle of affluent status groups. The Oldtowners benefit from improved community services, the increasing value of their property, and the enhanced positive image of Mobiltown as a community. Paradoxically, the status enhancement of Mobiltown, though causing more social divisions and segregation, has benefited most of the residents, old and new.

# 9

# The Outcomes of Status Enhancement: Implications of the "Settle with Us" Project

As a status enhancement scheme, the "settle with us" project in Mobiltown was aimed at two goals: attracting higher-status groups to an underprivileged community and achieving social integration between these newcomers and the veteran residents. Given that the newcomers were settled in their own neighborhoods and were capable of forming distinctive status groups, these two goals are at least partially contradictory. Our aim in this final chapter is to evaluate Mobiltown's experience in terms of its general implications. To what extent is the formation of neighborhood groups as status groups detrimental to social life in a community attempting status enhancement? In what sense can such a project achieve social integration?

## NEIGHBORHOOD GROUPS AS STATUS GROUPS

Prior to the "settle with us" project, Mobiltown was a socially and ethnically homogeneous town, fairly isolated from the rest of the country. In order to attract new residents of a higher SES and of the dominant Ashkenazi group, Mobiltown's leaders promised them their own neighborhoods. Actually, this is the essence of a status enhancement project in general: a lower-status community cannot expect voluntary immigration of higher-status groups without offering them special arrangements that will fit their lifestyle. The status enhancement of any given community depends on such voluntary immigration.

However, the price paid for the status ambitions of a community is neighborhood differentiation. In Mobiltown, as in any other mobile community, the qualitative difference in allegiance to the community is now imprinted in its ecological distribution into neighborhoods, which play a central role in the community structure. The division into neighborhoods renders other differences salient. Their socioeconomic and ethnic composition makes these neighborhoods tangible symbols. Because housing is one of the most expensive purchases in life, it represents one's socioeconomic standing more than other status symbols. A major aspect of the quality of housing is its location and immediate environment. Thus, the value of houses is generalized to the entire neighborhood.

The status connotation of neighborhoods is generated through the existence of social networks, common lifestyles, and collective interests vis-a-vis the community as a whole. From that perspective, we found it useful to concentrate on neighborhood groups rather than the larger ecological units of neighborhoods. The concept of neighborhood groups implies the breakdown of neighborhoods into social units according to fine SES distinctions, common lifestyles, and friendship networks, all of which dictate the sharing of interests. In a community undergoing status enhancement, neighborhood groups are often formed on the basis of ecological neighborhood coupled with the length of residence in the community. The length of residence, in this particular case, provides the SES distinctions necessary for the formation of neighborhood groups and supplies the basis for common lifestyles, friendships, and group interests.

Applying the concept of neighborhood groups to Mobiltown, we found, indeed, that many neighborhoods consist of separate groups, as indicated by their different lifestyles, friendship networks, perceptions, and attitudes. Thus, in contrast to the homogeneous military neighborhood, which constitutes a neighborhood group by itself, the civilian neighborhood of Newtown consists of two neighborhood groups: CIVILNEW and CIVILVET. While CIVILNEW is a group of mobile individuals who took advantage of the opportunity to fulfill their dreams of building luxurious houses, CIVILVET is the elite of old Mobiltown. As such, members of the latter are more strongly anchored in town, have friends there, and hold different outlooks on Mobiltown and on life in general. In Midtown and in Poortown, as well, we found that new and veteran residents formed separate neighborhood groups.

The way in which neighborhood groups establish their exclusive lifestyle and interests in the community is by forming themselves as status groups. A status group is defined by terms of inclusion and exclusion. Exclusive criteria may develop in both prestigious status groups and deprived and poor ones. The risk taken by any community attempting status enhancement is the development of its neighborhood groups into crystallized status groups. This process carries the potential of segregation and the supremacy of the particularistic interests that such groups may develop.

In general terms, all neighborhood groups are status groups in one way or another. The crystallization of a status group, however, is a function of its social development and structure, and one cannot assume that all neighborhoods experience the same degree of group formation despite differences in socioeconomic status and other social attributes. This is demonstrated in Mobiltown by the case of the veteran and newcomer groups in Midtown. MIDVET and MIDNEW remain relatively amorphous as status groups and are not recognized as cohesive groups either by themselves or by others.

On the other hand, we found several very cohesive status groups. MILIT, in particular, has become a major actor in the community scene and has developed its own organizational structure and leadership. It managed to achieve its particular interests in various life spheres—for example, community services, education, commercial and recreational facilities—by becoming a constant pressure group, which by now threatens the political power of the veteran leadership. Above and beyond the very crystallized attitudes and perceptions these newcomers have presented in the surveys, they developed a group self-image that emphasizes MILIT's "special contribution to the town." As a genuine status group—in Max Weber's original sense of the concept—it takes an active part in the public scene not only because of its particularistic interests, but also "for the good of the community." Consistent with this perception, this group often demonstrates disparaging attitudes toward Oldtowners, who are disdainfully labeled as "Mobiltowners." They refer to themselves as "the Neighborhood."

Those who are most hurt by the crystallization of the military families as a status group are the groups closest to them socially and geographically. These include, first of all, CIVILVET, which consists of the mobile Oldtowners. Social mobility and seniority in town are the basis of CIVILVET's definition as a status group and the reason for its ambivalent attitudes toward the newcomers. The fact that the veteran political elite, which constitutes an integral part of CIVILVET, may lose its powerful position due to MILIT's activity may explain this ambivalence.

Geographically close to MILIT, yet socially distant, is POORVET. The poverty and feelings of deprivation among this population have combined in its formation as a status group. The "settle with us" project has intensified the relative deprivation of this population, in reality and in their self-image. Though they may have benefited from improved services after the arrival of the newcomers, they have nevertheless demonstrated the most antagonistic attitudes toward Newtown.

It thus appears that status group distinctions in Mobiltown are central to its social and political life. Actually, the political struggle in Mobiltown, its commercial and cultural development, the changes in its educational system, and the perceptions of individual residents regarding themselves and others in the community cannot be explained without reference to the neighborhood groups as status groups. This consideration seems to be crucial for the comprehension of status enhancement projects.

## A NEW MEANING OF SOCIAL INTEGRATION

The prominence of the neighborhood groups as distinct status groups in all life aspects of Mobiltown raises the question of social integration. The notion of social integration between the higher-status newcomers and the lower-status veteran residents accompanied the "settle with us" project from its very early planning stages. Yet, as status groups focusing on exclusionary criteria, some neighborhood groups have pulled Mobiltown in the direction of segregation and potential conflict. To what extent can social integration be achieved under such circumstances?

The answer to this question seems to depend on the definition of social integration. The concept of social integration is intricate and carries various connotations, especially since it is used in various societies as an ideology-laden term representing the egalitarian goals of society. It has been used by politicians, public speakers, and the mass media as an ideological banner representing an ultimate solution to immanent conflicts among various social groups—mainly ethnic, racial, or religious groups characterized by relations of superordination versus subordination. Social integration, in such cases, is usually interpreted as a social goal, representing a utopian situation in which the various groups mix with each other and blend into one unified group.

Israel, as a society of immigrants, serves as a case in point for this ideological interpretation of the concept. The melting pot concept of *mizug galuyot* (literally, "blending of exiles"), used as an ideological banner by Israeli politicians during the early statehood years, was slowly replaced by the banner of "social integration." The latter is generally taken to mean the blending of lower-status Mizrachi Jews with higher-status Ashkenazim.

It is this ideological banner of social integration that was most often used by the veteran political elite of Mobiltown in the planning stages of the "settle with us" project. Their decision to wave this banner cannot be considered naive by any measure. First of all, they needed to "sell" to their veteran constituents a status enhancement project that would change the face of

Mobiltown dramatically—and what better way is there of selling such a project in a deprived development town than presenting it as serving the integrative ideology? Using this ideology also helped them secure the necessary resources and support of the national political establishment, especially the financial resources required for renovating Poortown neighborhoods at a later stage. It is also possible that the veteran political elite truly believed that the blending of newcomers and veterans was feasible, at least partially, because the lower-status veterans would be the "absorbers" of the higher-status group.

In any event, as time passed it became clear, both to the veteran elite and to all Mobiltowners, that the utopian notion of social integration had become an unrealistic goal of the project. Actually, the only veteran group that revealed some assimilatory tendencies toward the newcomers consisted of the veteran political elite and other mobile veterans, who moved into Newtown and built their houses in the new civilian neighborhood. The local political elite expected that a by-product of the status enhancement project would be an increase in their own status as local leaders and perhaps also in their position in the national political scene. However, although they remained the leaders, at least for the time being, they had to succumb to various particularistic interests of the newcomers. Most of these interests enhanced the segregation of the new neighborhood groups from the veteran ones. Hence, the legitimation of the project could no longer reside in the previously declared intention to implement social integration vis-a-vis the blending of new and veteran residents.

It is at this point that one wonders why the perceptions of most Mobiltowners regarding social integration in their town have remained positive. Our comparison of the first and second surveys reveals that despite the four years of segregative reality, both veterans and newcomers retained their positive attitudes toward the prospects of social integration in Mobiltown. Furthermore, they specifically agree that social integration has had a positive influence on most aspects of life in Mobiltown, with the exception of politics. In fact, their general satisfaction with life in Mobiltown has increased during this period.

To understand these seemingly paradoxical findings, one must resort to a different definition of the concept of social integration. Social integration can be defined from the viewpoint of its ultimate goal: raising the standard of living of the disadvantaged group and enhancing its life quality, life opportunities, and self-image. This goal may be achieved whether or not harmony is obtained between the privileged and deprived groups.

This is exactly what happened in Mobiltown as a result of the "settle with us" project. As a rule, the project set in motion a transformation of life patterns in the town that has affected all Mobiltowners. The new neighborhood groups have exerted the strongest influence on this transformation, and, subsequently, many of the cultural, educational, commercial, and social developments were based on some form of implicit segregation. Nevertheless, the life of Mobiltowners of all neighborhoods has changed.

The greatest achievement of the project has been the enhancement of the town's status. Mobiltown is no longer a "development town." Its public image has been upgraded, and its inhabitants are deeply aware of it. The market value of houses and apartments is on the rise, due to the demand of outsiders who want to settle in the town. Mobiltown attracts outsiders because it now possesses local institutions—educational, commercial, and cultural—and municipal services typical of a well-established community. The recent construction of a new road leading from the town to the Tel Aviv highway has brought Mobiltown physically closer to Israel's metropolitan center, and several industries opened local plants as a result of this development.

It is clear, therefore, why the general feeling of all Mobiltowners is that the town is now a better place to live in. The benefits of the town's status enhancement are, however, not evenly distributed among all Mobiltowners. Our findings definitely show that the stronger groups draw wider advantages. All groups, however, tend to recognize that the project has been beneficial. They seem to interpret the concept of social integration in terms of the increment in life quality of the veteran residents and their improved self-image as residents of Mobiltown. Though they are aware of the segregative tendencies of the new neighborhood groups and of their potential power as the future ruling elite in town, it seems that the shortcomings in this respect are not a major concern among Mobiltowners.

An answer to the question of whether social integration has been achieved by the "settle with us" project thus depends on how one interprets the concept. From the point of view of creating a homogeneous and harmonious community out of its various groups, the project has certainly fallen short of creating social integration. The project has created heterogeneity by allowing the establishment of segregative neighborhood groups and, moreover, has produced inequality by being overproportionally beneficial to the stronger and new groups. From the point of view of enhancing the life prospects and self-image of the less privileged group, however, the ultimate goals of social integration have been achieved, at least to some extent. Though the newcomers have benefited most, the veteran residents—at least in relative terms—have benefited too.

## FURTHER IMPLICATIONS OF MOBILTOWN'S EXPERIENCE

The program of social change implemented by Mobiltown grants the ensuing processes the quality of a quasi-laboratory experiment. As such, the "settle with us" project carries further implications—both for Israeli society in particular and for community change and renewal programs in general.

### Implications for Israeli Society

When we began our study, Mobiltown was one of many development towns built by the Israeli government in the 1950s in peripheral geographical areas, in order to absorb the immigrants from North Africa and the Middle East. In time, these development towns became symbols of the deprivation of Mizrachim in Israel. As such, many of their mayors gained power as symbolic leaders of the Mizrachi group and entered the national political scene, mainly as members of the Knesset, the Israeli parliament.

Gaining such power, many of them wanted to enhance the status of their own towns. This is how the "settle with us" project in Mobiltown started. Recently, the mayors of several other development towns, encouraged by Mobiltown's success story, have initiated similar projects in their own towns, attempting to attract higher-status and Ashkenazi inhabitants.

Since Mobiltown has become a model for imitation, it is important to understand its experience of status enhancement in general social terms. In Israeli society in general, mobile Mizrachim tend to assimilate into the Ashkenazi-dominated middle class (Ayalon, Ben-Rafael, and Sharot, 1988). As a result, ethnicity becomes an issue of less importance in the self-identity of the middle-class population.

The "settle with us" project actually attempted to turn Mobiltown into a middle-class community. Though some of the veteran residents remained deprived, the structural changes in Mobiltown have certainly turned it into an established middle-class community. One outcome of this trend is that Mobiltowners do not refer to ethnic terms in their perceptions of social gaps in their town. Status group competition has moved the ethnic factor to the background. In its struggle for a middle-class lifestyle, the social tensions typical of that lifestyle now tend to replace Mobiltown's past difficulties of isolation and marginality.

A related outcome concerns the mobile elements of Mobiltown's veteran population. A well-known problem of Israeli development towns is the out-migration of their mobile residents. Those who manage to attain higher education or to do well in business usually migrate from the development town to urban, middle-class centers. Consequently, they leave behind a community that continues to be characterized by poverty and deprivation, despite the social mobility of part of its population.

This has not happened in Mobiltown. To the contrary, the mobile elements here are capable of finding a middle-class social milieu among Newtowners. Hence, they do not feel the urge to leave the town. By staying in Mobiltown, they contribute to the status enhancement of the community, and they mitigate the social contrast between the new and veteran residents.

One possible consequence of copying Mobiltown's model in other development towns is the establishment of these towns as middle-class communities of a blurred ethnic identity. On one hand, this seems to be a successful solution to the persistent marginality of the development towns and to their severe problems of unemployment and out-migration. On the other hand, in the course of this process, the development towns may lose their edge as the representatives of the deprived Mizrachi group. Politically, the Mizrachim in Israel may lose the opportunity to present their interests in the national scene through the development towns and their leaders.

## Implications for Community Renewal

Its political implications notwithstanding, Mobiltown's experience presents a unique model of community renewal and social integration, applicable both to Israel and to other societies. Israel has attempted various experiments of residential integration between lower-status Mizrachim and higher-status Ashkenazim. Most of these experiments focused on resettling the lower-status group among a higher-status population or on the renewal of existing poor communities.

In other countries as well, much effort has been put into the renewal of deprived communities. Again, these efforts have mainly concentrated on attempts to revive the communities of poor minority groups through self-help schemes. In some cases, such communities were evacuated, and their inhabitants were resettled in more established communities, with the hope that their new environment might change their life perspectives and their actual opportunities. In some other cases, such as the Starrett City experiment in New York City and the Lake

Meadows and Prairie Shores developments in Chicago, attempts were made to integrate majority and minority groups in new neighborhoods through racial occupancy control programs aimed at balancing the ratios of the groups (Starr, 1985).

Most of these efforts have resulted in deep dissatisfaction of the parties involved. Community renewal projects have frequently led the local population to blame the "establishment," namely, the dominant ethnic group, for patronizing attitudes. The local inhabitants themselves became inactive in the self-help renovation schemes. Minority groups resettled in established neighborhoods have frequently encountered rejection on the part of the "absorbers." In any event, both partners of such integration schemes were dissatisfied.

What characterizes Mobiltown's experience is the general satisfaction of the residents with the project itself and with the positive effects of "social integration" on life in Mobiltown. We have attempted to explain these positive attitudes toward social integration, despite the obvious segregative tendencies, by the Mobiltowners' specific interpretation of the concept. Emphasizing the goals of integration, namely, improving the life prospects of the deprived groups, we see that the status enhancement of Mobiltown has, indeed, apparently benefited all its residents.

One may wonder why Mobiltown's experience has led to such satisfaction, while other experiments of community renewal or social integration have not. After all, renewal projects and the resettlement of minority groups may also enhance the life prospects of the deprived group. In principle, they should lead to similar satisfaction.

It seems that the answer lies in the unique circumstances of Mobiltown's experiment. Of particular importance are three factors. First, the lower-status veteran population, rather than a dominant "establishment," initiated the project and invited the higher-status group to settle with them. Second, this lower-status group enjoyed some advantages due to its seniority in town, and the contact with the newcomers could not have destroyed its self-image despite the apparent socioeconomic gaps.

Third, the higher-status group voluntarily settled in Mobiltown and therefore could not totally reject the lower-status group, although it attempted to segregate itself.

As for the newcomers, their overproportionate benefits from the project and their awareness of their contribution to the town explain their satisfaction and positive attitudes toward social integration. The positive perceptions of the veteran residents may be explained by the special circumstances listed above. The veterans became fully aware of the segregative tendencies of the newcomers and of the slim chances to achieve social integration in the sense of blending. Their recognition that the newcomers will rule Mobiltown in the near future indicates this awareness. However, they had no outside "establishment" to blame for this development, nor did the segregation of the newcomers dramatically hurt their own self-image. So, instead of complaining, they preferred to look on the positive side of the irreversible reality and redefine social integration in terms of their own benefits from the project. This way, the unique circumstances of Mobiltown's experience ensured that both the strong and the weak partners of the scheme remained satisfied.

This general satisfaction of all groups of residents makes Mobiltown's experience an attractive model for the renewal of communities of underprivileged minorities. It seems that it may be preferable to the common models of community renewal or social integration. The Mobiltown model ensures true status enhancement of the entire community, from which everyone benefits. However, communities wishing to adopt this model should be aware of its painstaking consequences. First, in order to attract higher-status groups to the deprived community, they must allocate to them the resources required for maintaining their lifestyle and even improving it. Second, they cannot expect in return that the newcomers will reciprocate by blending in and accepting the veteran leadership. On the contrary, they will probably attempt to segregate themselves and challenge the local political elite. Thus, the local leadership inviting such newcomers to "settle with us" should be aware that it may be committing political suicide.

The only benefit that should be expected by adopting the Mobiltown model is status enhancement, which is the essence of community renewal. Even this, however, is a painstaking process. The newcomers' share in the benefits of the status enhancement process is bound to be larger than that of the veterans, and the latter should be ready to accept this. Above all, they should realize that the newcomers' arrival does not merely add a new component to the community. Once the status enhancement project is set in motion, life patterns in the community are going to change forever. The community experiencing status enhancement becomes a new community, and the process is irreversible.

# Appendix: Methodology

## DISCRIMINANT ANALYSIS

Discriminant analysis (Klecka, 1980) exerts the functions or dimensions that separate a set of nominal categories (groups) according to a predetermined set of interval variables (the discriminating variables). There are two possible types of relations between the discriminating variables and the nominal variable. First, the nominal variable can be treated as dependent upon the interval variables. In this form, discriminant analysis parallels multiple regression. Second, the interval variables may be defined as dependent upon the group. This form produces an extension of multivariate analysis of variance.

In our study, the discriminant analysis takes the second form, with the neighborhood groups as the nominal categories. Combinations of variables that pertain to behaviors, attitudes, and perceptions constitute the discriminant functions.

The discriminating power of a function is obtained by the canonical correlation, which summarizes the degree of association between the groups and the discriminant function. The canonical correlation, always positive, ranges from 0 (no association) to 1 (perfect association).

The statistical significance of the function is tested by Wilks' Lambda. Wilks' Lambda tests the residual discrimination in the system prior to deriving the function. Lambda is an "inverse" measure—as it increases toward its maximum level (1.00), it reports diminishing discrimination. Lambda can be converted into an approximation of chi-square and hence serves as a test of significance.

The substantive interpretation of the function is based on the standardized discriminant function coefficients. These indicate the relative importance of each interval variable in distinguishing among the categories of the nominal variable (in our study, the various neighborhood groups). The larger the magnitude of a standardized coefficient, the greater is the variable's contribution to the discriminating power of the function.

The relative positions of the various groups are summarized by the groups' centroids. These are the mean function scores on each nominal category (in our example, the means on the various neighborhood groups). The coupling of the standardized discriminant function coefficients and the centroids enables the interpretation of the pattern of the relationship, including its direction.

## THE LINEAR STRUCTURAL RELATIONS MODEL

The linear structural relations model (Wold, 1982; Zak, 1981) incorporates unmeasured constructs (or latent variables) in a path analytical model. The various coefficients are estimated by a partial least square solution (PLS). PLS estimates simultaneously the relationship between the latent variables (the path coefficients) and those between each latent variable and its indicators.

The weights of the indicators constructing each latent variable are estimated in either of two methods: a factor analytical procedure or a regression procedure. The first method is known as the outwardly directed model. It assumes that each latent variable is a factor that serves as a predictor of its indicators. Consequently, the coefficients of the outward model are parallel to factor loadings. Most of the latent variables in our analyses are outwardly directed. The outwardly directed latent variables are portrayed in our models by arrows directed from the construct (represented by encircled names) to its indicators (represented by rectangles).

In the inwardly directed model, the latent variable is regressed on its indicators. Hence, the latent variable is a transformed composite variable of a set of indicator variables, and the coefficients are interpreted as regression betas. We use this method, which is less common, for the construction of the neighborhood groups construct. The various neighborhood groups are represented by a set of dummy variables (MIDNEW serves as the reference group, and the respective dummy variable is omitted from the analysis). We use the inwardly directed model for the construction of this latent variable since we see no point in assuming that neighborhood is a factor that predicts its indicator. Due to the same reasoning we decided against the use of the better-known method for path analysis with latent variables—LISREL (Joreskog, 1978), which does not permit the incorporation of an inwardly directed model.

So far, we have referred to the outer part of the linear structural relation model (the measurements model), which describes the relationships between the latent variables and their indicators. The other part of the model is the inner part (the structural relations), which describes the relationships between the latent variables. The relations among the various factors that comprise the inner part of the model (in our models the inner part consists of both latent variables and ordinary manifest variables; the incorporation of the latter in the linear structural relations model is quite common) are given by path coefficients. The path coefficients are presented in our models by the figures attached to the respective arrows. The interpretation of the relationships in the inner model is the same as for ordinary regression results.

# References


Alterman, R. and M. Hill. 1988. "Evaluating the Decentralization Policy of Israel's Project Renewal: Paradoxes of Implementation in a Highly-Centralized State." *Megamot* 31: 322-341 (in Hebrew).

Arzi, Y., and Y. Amir. 1976. "Personal Adjustment and Scholastic Gains of Culturally Deprived Children in Homogeneous and Heterogeneous Classrooms." *Megamot* 22: 279-287 (in Hebrew).

Ayalon, H., E. Ben-Rafael, and S. Sharot. 1986. "The Costs and Benefits of Ethnic Identification." *British Journal of Sociology* 37: 550-568.

Ayalon, H., E. Ben-Rafael, and S. Sharot. 1988. "The Impact of Stratification: Assimilation or Ethnic Solidarity." In A. L. Kalleberg, ed., *Research in Social Stratification and Mobility,* Vol. 7, pp. 305-326. Greenwich, CT: JAI Press.

Badie, B., and P. Birnbaum. 1983. *The Sociology of the State.* Chicago: University of Chicago Press.

Balakrishnan, T. R. 1976. "Ethnic Residential Segregation in the Metropolitan Areas of Canada." *Canadian Journal of Sociology* 1: 481-498.

Balakrishnan, T. R. 1982. "Changing Patterns of Ethnic Residential Segregation in the Metropolitan Areas of Canada." *Canadian Review of Sociology and Anthropology* 19: 92-110.

Ben-Rafael, E. 1982. *The Emergence of Ethnicity: Cultural Groups and Social Conflict in Israel.* Westport, CT: Greenwood Press.

Ben-Rafael, E. 1985. "Ethnicity -- Theory and Myth." *Megamot* 29: 190-204 (in Hebrew).

Berger, B. M. 1960. *Working-Class Suburb: A Study of Auto Workers in Suburbia.* Berkeley: University of California Press.

Berry, B. J. L., C. A. Goodwin, R. W. Lake and K. B. Smith. 1976. "Attitudes Toward Integration: The Role of Status in Community Response to Racial Change." In B. Shwartz, ed., *The Changing Face of the Suburb,* pp. 221-264. Chicago: University of Chicago Press.

Blass, N., and B. Amir. 1984. "Integration in Education: The Development of a Policy." In Y. Amir and S. Sharan, eds., *School Desegregation: Cross-Cultural Perspectives,* pp. 63-98. Hillsdale, NJ: Erlbaum Associates.

Bourdieu, P., and J. C. Passeron. 1977. *Reproduction in Education, Society and Culture.* London: Sage Publications.

Brewer, M. B., and R. M. Kramer. 1985. "The Psychology of Intergroup Attitudes and Behavior." *Annual Review of Psychology* 36: 219-243.

Brewer, M. B., and N. Miller. 1984. "Beyond the Contact Hypothesis: Theoretical Perspectives on Desegregation." In N. Miller and M. Brewer, eds., *Groups in Contact: The Psychology of Desegregation,* pp. 281-302. New York: Academic Press.

Butler, D. and D. Stokes. 1974. *Political Change in Britain: The Evolution of Electoral Choice.* New York: St. Martin's.

Carmon, N. 1988. "Deliberate Social Change: Evaluation of Israel's Project Renewal." *Megamot* 31: 299-321 (in Hebrew).

Chen, M., A. Lewy, and D. Kfir. 1977. "The Possibilities of Interethnic Group Contact in the Junior High Schools: Implementations and Results." *Megamot* 23: 101-123 (in Hebrew).

Churchman, A. 1987. "Can Resident Participation in Neighborhood Rehabilitation Succeed? Israel's Project Renewal Through a Comparative Perspective." In I. Altman and A. Wandersman, eds., *Neighborhood and Community Environments,* Vol. 9, pp. 113-162. New York: Plenum Press.

Colbjornsen, T. 1988. "Organizing Collective Interests: Causes of Cross-National Differences in Working-Class Formation." In A. L. Kalleberg, ed., *Research in Social Stratification and Mobility,* Vol. 7, pp. 147-272. Greenwich, CT: JAI Press.

Coleman, J. S., S. D. Kelly, and J. A. Moore. 1975. *Trends in School Segregation, 1968-73*. Washington, D C: Urban Institute.

Collins, R. 1975. *Conflict Sociology: Toward an Explanatory Science*. New York: Academic Press.

Collins, R. 1979. *The Credential Society: An Historical Sociology of Education and Stratification.* New York: Academic Press.

Collins, R. 1986. *Max Weber: A Skeleton Key*. Beverly Hills, CA: Sage Publications.

Collver, A., and M. Semyonov. 1979. "Suburban Change and Persistence." *American Sociological Review* 44: 480-486.

Daalder, H. 1966. "Parties, Elites and Political Development in Western Europe." In J. La Palombara and M. Weiner, eds., *Political Parties and Political Development,* Pp. 43-77. Princeton, NJ: Princeton University Press.

Dahl, K. A. 1961. *Who Governs? Democracy and Power in an American City*. New Haven, CT: Yale University Press.

Darroch, A. G., and W. G. Marston. 1971. "The Social Class Basis of Ethnic Residential Segregation: The Canadian Case." *American Journal of Sociology* 77: 491-510.

Davis, J. A., J. L. Spaeth, and C. Huson. 1961. "Analyzing Effects of Group Composition." *American Sociological Review* 26: 215-225.

DiMaggio, P. 1982. "Cultural Capital and School Success: The Import of Status Culture Participation on the Grades of U.S. High School Students." *American Sociological Review* 47: 189-201.

Efrat, E. 1987. *Development Towns in Israel: Past or Future?* Tel Aviv: Achiasaf (in Hebrew).

Foladare, I. S. 1968. "The Effect of Neighborhood on Voting Behavior." *Political Science Quarterly* 83: 516-529.

Frank, L., and L. Dobson. 1985. "Interest Groups: The Problem of Representation." *Western Political Quarterly* 38: 224-237.

Gabriel, S., M. Justman, and A. Levy. 1986. "An Integrative Analysis of Migration, Investment and Unemployment in Israeli New Towns." *Economic Quarterly* 36: 513-521 (in Hebrew).

Gans, H. J. 1961. "The Balanced Community." *Journal of American Institute of Planners* 27: 176-184.

Gans, H. J. 1967. *The Levittowners: Ways of Life and Politics in a New Suburban Community*. New York: Pantheon.

Gerrard, H. B., and N. Miller, eds. 1975. *School Desegregation*. New York: Plenum Press.

Glaser, N. 1975. *Affirmative Discrimination, Ethnic Inequality, and Public Policy*. New York: Basic Books.

Guest, A. M. 1978. "Suburban Social Status: Persistence or Evolution?" *American Sociological Review* 43: 251-264.

Guest, A. M., and J. A. Weed. 1976. "Ethnic Residential Segregation: Patterns of Change." *American Journal of Sociology* 81: 1088-1111.

Hartman, M. 1979. "Prestige Grading of Occupations with Sociologists as Judges." *Quality and Quantity* 13: 1-19.

Hewstone, M., and R. Brown. 1986. "Contact Is Not Enough: An Intergroup Perspective on the Contact Hypothesis." In M. Hewstone and R. Brown, eds., *Contact and Conflict in Intergroup Encounters,* pp. 1-44. New York: Blackwell.

Huckfeldt, R. R. 1983. "Social Contexts, Social Networks, and Urban Neighborhoods: Environmental Constraints on Friendship Choice." *American Journal of Sociology* 89: 651-669.

Huckfeldt, R. R. 1986. *Politics in Context: Assimilation and Conflict in Urban Neighborhoods*. New York: Agathon Press.

Jones, F. L. 1967. "Ethnic Concentration and Assimilation: An Australian Case Study." *Social Forces* 45: 412-423.

Joreskog, K. G. 1978. "Structural Analysis of Covariance and Correlation Matrices." *Psychometrica* 43: 443-477.

Kantrowitz, N. 1981. "Ethnic Segregation: Social Reality and Academic Myth." In C. Peach, V. Robinson and S. Smith, eds., *Ethnic Segregation in Cities,* pp. 43-57. London: Croom Helm.

Katznelson, I., and A.R. Zolberg, eds. 1986. *Working Class Formation*. Princeton, NJ: Princeton University Press.

Klaff, V. Z. 1973. "Ethnic Segregation in Urban Israel." *Demography* 10: 161-184.

Klaff, V. Z. 1977. "Residence and Integration in Israel: A Mosaic of Segregated People." *Ethnicity* 4: 103-121.

Klecka, W. R. 1980. *Discriminant Analysis*. London: Sage.

Kraus, V. 1984. "Social Segregation in Israel as a Function of Objective and Subjective Attributes of the Ethnic Groups." *Sociology and Social Research* 69: 50-71.

Kraus, V., and Y. Koresh. 1992. "The Course of Residential Segregation: Ethnicity, Socioeconomic Status and Suburbanization in Israel." *Sociological Quarterly* 33: 303-319.

Kweit, M., and R. Kweit. 1981. *Implementing Citizen Participation in a Bureaucratic Society*. New York: Praeger.

Landsberger, H. 1980. "The Trend Toward Citizens' Participation in the Welfare State: Countervailing Power to the Professions." In C. Foster, ed., *Comparative Public Policy and Citizen Participation,* pp. 228-243. New York: Pergamon Press.

Lazerwitz, B. 1985. "Class, Ethnicity, and Site as Planning Factors in Israeli Residential Integration." *International Review of Modern Sociology* 15: 23-43.

Lockwood, D. 1966. "Sources of Variation in Working Class Images of Society." *Sociological Review* 14: 249-267.

Logan, J. R. 1978. "Growth, Politics, and the Stratification of Places." *American Journal of Sociology* 84: 404-415.

Logan, J. R., and H. L. Molotch. 1987. *Urban Fortunes: The Political Economy of Place.* Berkeley: University of California Press.

Logan, J. R., and M. Schneider. 1981. "The Stratification of Metropolitan Suburbs: 1969-1970." *American Sociological Review* 46: 175-186.

Long, M. E. 1958. "The Local Community as an Ecology of Games." *American Journal of Sociology* 44: 251-261.

Marans, R. 1978. "Kiryat Gat, Israel: A New Town." In *The Role of Housing in Promoting Social Integration,* pp. 79-127. New York: Department of Economic and Social Affairs, United Nations.

Massey, D. S. 1985. "Ethnic Residential Segregation: A Theoretical Synthesis and Empirical Review." *Sociology and Social Research* 72: 58-67.

Massey, D. S., and N. A. Denton. 1988. "Spatial Assimilation as a Socioeconomic Outcome." *American Sociological Review* 50: 94-106.

Mercer, J. R., P. Iadicola, and H. Moore. 1986. "Building Effective Multiethnic Schools: Evolving Models and Paradigms." In W. G. Stephan and J. R. Feagin, eds., *School Desegregation: Past, Present and Future,* pp. 281-307. New York: Plenum Press.

Mills, C. W. 1956. *The Power Elite.* New York: Oxford University Press.

Molotch, H. L. 1973. *Managed Integration: Dilemmas of Doing Good to the City.* Berkeley: University of California Press.

Molotch, H. L. 1976. "The City as a Growth Machine: Toward a Political Economy of Place." *American Journal of Sociology* 82: 309-332.

Orbell, J. M., and K. S. Sherrill. 1969. "Racial Attitudes and the Metropolitan Context: A Structural Analysis." *Public Opinion Quarterly* 33: 46-54.

Park, R. E., E. W. Burgess, and R. D. McKenzie. 1925. *The City*. Chicago: University of Chicago Press.

Peerce, D. M. 1981. "Deciphering the Dynamics of Segregation: The Role of School in the Housing Choice Process." *The Urban Review* 13: 85-101.

Peres, Y. 1976. *Ethnic Relations in Israel.* Tel Aviv: Sifriyat Hapoalim (in Hebrew).

Pettigrew, T. R. 1973. "Attitudes on Race and Housing: A Social Psychological View." In A. H. Hawley and V. P. Rock, eds., *Segregation in Residential Areas,* pp. 21-84. Washington, D. C.: National Academy of Sciences.

Prysby, C. L. 1975. "Neighborhood Class Composition and Individual Partisan Choice: A Test with Chilean Data." *Social Science Quarterly* 56: 225-238.

St. John, N. H. 1975. *School Desegregation Outcomes for Children.* New York: Wiley.

Sarkisean, W. 1976. "The Idea of Social Mix in Town Planning: A Historical Review." *Urban Studies* 13: 231-246.

Schwarzwald, J., and Y. Amir. 1984. "Interethnic Relations and Education: An Israeli Perspective." In N. Miller and M.B. Brewer, eds., *Groups in Contact: Psychology of Desegregation,* pp. 53-76. New York: Academic Press.

Segal, D. R., and S. H. Wildstrom. 1970. "Community Effects on Political Attitudes: Partisanship and Efficacy." *Sociological Quarterly* 11: 67-86.

Semyonov, M., and V. Kraus. 1982. "Thee Social Hierarchies of Communities and Neighborhoods." *Social Science Research* 63: 780-789.

Semyonov, M., and A. Tyree. 1981. "Community Segregation and the Costs of Ethnic Subordination." *Social Forces* 59: 649-666.

Shuval, J. 1962. "The Micro-Neighborhood: An Approach to Ecological Patterns of Ethnic Groups." *Social Problems* 9: 272-280.

Sliefer, Y., and A. Stoup. 1981. *A Plan for Urban Development.* Jerusalem: Ministry of Construction, Division of Programming (in Hebrew).

Smooha, S. 1978. *Israel: Pluralism and Conflict.* London: Routledge & Kegan Paul.

Smooha, S. 1984. "Three Perspectives in the Sociology of Ethnic Relations in Israel." *Megamot* 28: 169-206 (in Hebrew).

Spilerman, S., and J. Habib. 1976. "Development Towns in Israel: The Role of Community in Creating Ethnic Disparities in Labor Force Characteristics." *American Journal of Sociology* 81: 781-812.

Spiro, S. E. 1988. "Issues in the Evaluation of Neighborhood Rehabilitation Programs: Lessons from Israel's Project Renewal." *Megamot* 31: 269-285 (in Hebrew).

Stahura, J. M. 1986. "Black Suburbanization." *American Sociological Review* 51: 131-144.

Stahura, J. M. 1987. "Suburban Socioeconomic Status Change." *American Sociological Review* 52: 268-277.

Starr, R. 1985. "Racial Occupancy Controls." In *Issues of Housing Discrimination,* Vol. 1, pp. 145-155. Washington, DC: United States Commission on Civil Rights.

State of Israel. 1977. *Social Profile of Cities and Towns in Israel.* Part 2. Jerusalem: Ministry of Social Welfare, Division of Planning (in Hebrew).

Stephan, W. G., and J. R. Feagin, eds. 1986. *School Desegregation: Past Present and Future.* New York: Plenum Press.

Stoup, A. 1983. "The Attraction of New Population to an Underprivileged Settlement." *Environmental Planning* 30: 15-28 (in Hebrew).

Swirski, S. 1981. *'Lo Nechshalim Ela Menuchshalim' (Orientals and Ashkenazim in Israel: The Ethnic Division of Labor).* Haifa: Machbarot Le'Mechkar U'Lebikoret (in Hebrew).

Tauber, K. E. 1979. "Housing, Schools and Incremental Segregative Effects." *Annals of the American Academy of Political and Social Sciences* 441: 157-167.

Van Valey, T. L., W. C. Roof, and J. E. Wilcox. 1977. "Trends in Residential Segregation: 1969-1970." *American Journal of Sociology* 82: 826-844.

Weber, M. 1946. "Class, Status, Party." In H. H. Gerth and C. W. Mills, eds., *From Max Weber: Essays in Sociology,* pp. 180-195. New York: Oxford University Press.

Weintraub, D., and V. Kraus. 1982. "Social Differentiation and Locality of Residence: Spatial Distribution, Composition, and Stratification in Israel." *Megamot* 27: 367-381 (in Hebrew).

Wilson, R. A. 1971. "Anomie in the Ghetto: A Study of Neighborhood Type, People, and Anomie." *American Journal of Sociology* 77: 66-68.

Wirth, L. 1938. "Urbanism as a Way of Life." *American Journal of Sociology* 44: 1-24.

Wold, H. 1982. "Soft Modelling: The Basic Design and Some Extensions." In K. G. Joreskog and H. Wold, eds., *Systems Under Indirect Observation: Structure Prediction Causality,* pp. 1-54. Amsterdam: North Hilland.

Wooton, G. 1985. *Interest Groups, Policy and Politics in America.* Engelwood Cliffs, NJ: Prentice-Hall.

Wright, G. C. 1977. "Contextual Models of Electoral Behavior: The Southern Wallace Vote." *American Political Science Review* 71: 497-508.

Yogev, A. 1981. "Determinants of Early Educational Career in Israel: Further Evidence for the Sponsorship Thesis." *Sociology of Education* 54: 181-194.

Yogev, A. 1989a. "Educational Policy in Israel Toward the Advancement of Weak Student Populations." In *The Planning of Educational Policy: Position Papers and Decisions of the Steering Committee of the Pedagogic Secretariat,* pp. 175-205. Jerusalem: Ministry of Education and Culture (in Heberw).

Yogev, A. 1989b. "From School Reform to Ethnic Integration in Israeli Schools: Social Myths and Educational Policy." In A. Yogev and S. Tomlinson, eds., *International Perspectives on Education and Society* , Vol. 1, pp. 63-79. Greenwich, CT: JAI Press.

Yogev A., and H. Ayalon. 1986. "High School Attendance in a Sponsored Multi-Ethnic System: The Case of Israel." In A. C. Kerckhoff, ed., *Research in Sociology of Education and Socialization,* Vol. 6, pp. 79-101. Greenwich, CT: JAI Press.

Yogev, A., and S. Tomlinson, eds. 1989. *Affirmative Action and Positive Policies in the Education of Ethnic Minorities.* Vol. 1 of *International Perspectives on Education and Society.* Greenwich, CT: JAI Press.

Zak, I. 1981. "Latent Variables in Causal Models: An Example from Educational Research." In A. Lewy and S. Kugelmas, eds., *Decision Oriented Evaluation in Education: The Case of Israel,* pp. 195-214. Philadelphia: International Science Services.

# Index

**About the Authors**

HANNA AYALON is Senior Lecturer at the School of Education and Department of Sociology and Anthropology, Tel Aviv University.

ELIEZER BEN-RAFAEL is Associate Professor in the Department of Sociology at Tel Aviv University.

ABRAHAM YOGEV is Associate Professor at the School of Education and Department of Sociology and Anthropology, Tel Aviv University.